Creative Approaches to

CHILD DEVELOPMENT
with MUSIC, LANGUAGE
and MOVEMENT

A RARE MOMENT OF QUIET—Mrs. Nash (standing) explains to her students the creative approach to teaching music.

MOVING TO THE MUSIC—Music teachers experience the importance of movement to understanding music.

Creative Approaches to

CHILD DEVELOPMENT
with MUSIC, LANGUAGE
and MOVEMENT

By GRACE C. NASH

Edited by J. ROBERT WELSH

Alfred Publishing Co., Inc.

Library of Congress Catalog Card Number: 73-93672
ISBN: 0-88284-014-2

Printed in the United States of America

Contents

Foreword

Music expressed in speech and song, with hands and feet, with easy-to-play beautifully toned instruments is exhilarating and exciting. Making music with others is much better than making it alone. Brainstorming and cooperating to build an ensemble can bring excellence and beauty that is unreachable by oneself.

This book deals with the whys, hows, and ingredients of active music-making with the voice, the body, and classroom instruments in a variety of textures and registers. Rather than imposing an adult concept of music on the student, I am concerned with the child's nature—his way of solving problems, his native tools and endowments of curiosity and reasoning, of moving and reaching—and his needs for worthiness and achievement.

As his space becomes smaller, his need for flexibility increases—to be able to live and communicate peacefully with others, to work with others for mutual benefit of earth and man. No longer can he live in a self-centered individual world.

In our open space schools where much of the day is spent in individual pursuits, music-making has become a vital daily need. Daily practice in such working together and listening to each other is a human need. Deprived of such brainstorming and "peak" experiences, one soon loses the desire for anything greater than that which he can achieve by himself. The exhilaration that comes with "self-stretching" to meet performance skills in group effort does not occur and the student goes his own way, becoming more self-centered and less concerned with the needs of others.

The new role of the arts, and music *per se,* in elementary education is focusing on greater individual effort, more creativity in self expression, release from tensions through rhythmic motor-muscular response and basic performance skills. These goals can be attained in a greater degree through active involvement with the ingredients of music, language and movement, rather than a "talking about" and "listening to" program in the traditional manner. And, if American education in its various forms is dealing with human needs, then active music-making in class size and/or smaller groups is needed more often and more than ever before in order to counteract and balance the increasing amount of packaged and individual learning that fills the rest of the day.

This puts music at the core of the curriculum, and in relationship to human disciplines, at the core of human development.

Acknowledgments

This is to express appreciation and acknowledgments to colleagues and authorities in music and related fields for their contributions, guidance, opportunities, and inspiration received in the development and application of this approach to child development:

Dr. Herbert Zipper, Director of Projects, University of Southern California
Louise Ide Burge, Professional Flautist, Music Center of the North Shore, Winnetka, Illinois
J. Robert Welsh, Editor-Author, "Making Music At the Keyboard"
Glen Fifield, Music Education, Utah State University, Logan, Utah
The late Blaine Blonquist, Music Director, Ogden City Schools, Ogden, Utah
Mary Osborne, Principal, Middlefork School, Northfield, Illinois
Barbara Andress, Arizona State University; former Music Coordinator, Cartwright School
    District, Phoenix, Arizona
Dr. Bickley Simpson, Research Specialist, Behavioral Sciences, Milton, Massachusetts
Grant Beglarian, Dean of Fine Arts, University of Southern California
Dr. Lloyd Schmidt, Music Consultant, State Department of Education, Hartford, Connect-
    icutt

Music Specialists: Murray McNair, Shore Country Day School, Beverly, Mass.
    Jeanne Loudon, Winchester Public Schools, Mass.
    Janice Rapley, San Francisco Public Schools, Calif.
    Sr. Conleth Hager, St. Peter Convent School, St. Paul, Minn.
    Marshia Beck, Orinda, California

Classroom teachers: Minerva Cook, Lowell School, Mesa, Ariz.
    Marie Pyer, Madison School, Madera, Calif.
    Pearl McGinnis, Madera, Calif.

And, for the learning received from the educational works of:
Carl Orff, Gunild Keetmann, Doreen Hall (Orff Schulwerk) and their exponents;
The late Zoltan Kodaly of Hungary and his exponents including, Arpad Darazs, Director
    of Choral Studies, University of South Carolina, Columbia, S.C.
The late Rudolf Laban of England and his exponents including, Vera Gray, BBC, London,
    England.

GRACE C. NASH

CHAPTER 1

Today With Music: Perspectives

> The function of beauty in the education of children is to lead them imperceptibly to love through sensory experiencing what they will afterwards learn to know in its own form as an intelligible principle.
>
> —Plato

OVERVIEW

Today with Music is an approach to child development through the components of music combined with language and movement, rather than the teaching of music as a subject and/or imposing an adult concept of music on the child. This approach uses the elements of music, namely rhythm and melody, expressed in different textures (timbres) and registers, together with language and movement according to the child's world. His way of learning and his needs in this changing environment are primary considerations.

Process

The process is one of building an ensemble from a small idea or sound into extensions and complexities through contributions, cooperation, and collaboration with others. Where it may start with a simple rhyme, experience or fantasy, the ensemble expands into other media of sound, color, movement, and language in a gestalt-like growth. The participants explore possibilities, using no less than three of their senses (sight, touch-manipulation and hearing) which can be extended into peripheral sensory intake. They become more alive and alert, more able and flexible in solving problems. As they become more selective and discriminating in their judgments, they are also finding out about themselves in relation to the environment.

Purpose

Where the purpose and concern are for the total growth of the child, rather than his acquiring a particular performance skill and musical knowledge, the outcome is a higher degree of skill and knowledge that are basic to all musical performance, and a greater sensitivity to his total environment.

Sources

The sources of this philosophy can be found in the educational premises and philosophies of a number of master minds,[1] defined and combined according to the nature and needs of children in America; enhanced and clarified by these children's interpretations and extensions; substantiated by continuing experience with children and teachers, together with probing research in the behavioral sciences.

EXPOSITION

Active learning

Active learning takes place:
- when the individual sees relevance to his world in the subject matter or problem at hand;
- when the media are acceptable to his nature and needs;
- when involvement engages the faculties, and emotions;
- when the goal or media appear so desirable that failure is no deterrent to his participation, but rather a motivation to try again;
- when the media offer reason to contribute his ideas, to listen to others, and to participate;
- when the result holds achievement and knowledge that he esteems for himself.

Play techniques

This approach is directed toward such active learning by utilizing the elements and techniques found in *play:* where the child learns the fastest; is the most creative and flexible; where failure is no deterrent to trying again; where his interactions are provocative and joyous; where problem-solving takes place through testing and evaluating; where the game at hand can stop at any point to be continued later—flexibility.

Play contains strong elements of *repetition* essential to the child's security. Within this repetition there will be differences in starting points, in patterns, climaxes, endings and extensions.

Rhythmic expression

Expressing rhythm is part of the nature of childhood. Rhythm is the organizing factor in his play. Rhythm can be the same joyous force in classroom learning.

Language

In this approach there is a feast of language enjoyment before and after the child starts to read. He makes the rhythms of words come alive as he rolls them on his tongue, tasting and feeling them in his mouth, as in: "Hickory, dickory," "Lolla pallooza Kalamazoo, marshmallow, cinnamon, lollypop stick," "Deedle, deedle dumpling," "Yuk, guck, mudpuddle, splash, ooh, zing!" Gobbledy gook language, nursery rhymes, sayings and riddles—these are his illusions of life, his "inside" reality and fantasy which prepare him for the adult world of reality. Expressing them with rhythmic flow, accents, different

[1] Herbert Zipper, U.S.A., Director of Projects, University of Southern California; educator; conductor, symphony and opera; Carl Orff, Germany, master composer-educator; author of the Orff Schulwerk (Music For Children Series) (translation by Doreen Hall and Arnold Walter, Canada); Zoltan Kodaly, Hungary, the late master composer-educator and author of Musica Hungarica Choral Series; Rudolf Laban, England, the late founder and author of Laban School of Dance, Ballet Notation System, Science of Motion; and his exponents, Ann Driver, Rachel Percival and Vera Gray. (Some of the movement principles found in both the Orff Schulwerk and the Laban Schools have their sources in Dalcroze Eurhythmics.)

voice levels and body actions, increases his enjoyment and awareness of language. Adding tonal textures to the ensemble heightens the acuity of all five senses.

Ostinato

This is a repeated pattern in sound, language or action, usually rhythmic by nature of its repetition.

The need for repetition in childhood experience is found in their repeated patterns of speech (from inflected gurgling sounds in infancy into words and phrases). These short repeated patterns called "ostinati" (ostinato, singular) are also a device in musical composition. Their repeated sound patterns (spoon tapping, drumming, skating a stick along a railing) and their repeated action patterns (hopping on one foot, hand clapping, foot tapping) bring rhythm into their performance, which generates organization and form. That children are born organizers; that rhythm is their chief tool and stabilizer; these facts are revealed again and again in their play.

Elemental music?

Out of this instinctive involvement with rhythm and melody comes the term "elemental music," a major tenet in the Orff Schulwerk.

Where the elemental forces in nature are sun, wind and rain, the elemental forces in music are rhythm and melody, qualities that are inherent in man and therefore are needed by him and expressed in his language, movements and feelings. In elemental music the melody is more often improvised, growing out of chants and calls that stem from the universal chant of three tones, So-Mi-La, and accompanied by rhythmic ostinati which are also melodic in their bordun-like character—fourths and fifths in patterns and/or parallel motion. Each small pattern has substance and character of its own. The interaction or ensemble builds differently with each repetition. It is open ended, always in a state of growth-enhancement according to the changes and contributions made by the participants.

Harmonic structure is not a function in elemental music, nor do harmonic modulations occur within a song or piece. Yet the different ostinati together make a consonant and rich total sound against the longer improvised song-melody that may be harmonic in texture and feeling.

For the child, elemental music is his way of making music and is a direct route to his understanding the *art form* in music. With his rhythms and chants that he uses in *play,* he makes his ensemble, which grows in its complexities as he grows in language, coordination and exploration of sound textures. He is listening, exploring, manipulating and experiencing. He *is* the composer, the performer and the listener! It is "here and now" music. Skills used and developed in elemental music making are basic to all musical performance. The musical forms developed (canon, rondo, variations, etc.) are common to *art forms* of any period. The working-with sound textures in language, instruments and movement extend his faculties toward peripheral sensory intake so that he is capable of listening to larger works in art form with increasing comprehension.

Although notation is not a segment of elemental music, the rhythmic speech and song patterns, instrumental ostinati and improvisations, together with motor experiences —all these clarify and prepare for notation in a phrase translation rather than halting note-to-note reading. This phrase transition into notation substantiates one of the premises of Orff: that speech exercise stands at the beginning of all musical exercise, rhythmic as well as melodic.

Analysis of rhythm

There are four aspects of rhythm defined and described by Ray Barsch[1] as
1) rhythm of the cosmos (day and night, seasons, rotation of the earth, etc.)
2) biologic rhythm (heart beat, blood circulation, digestive system, etc.)
3) performance rhythm (motor enactment)
4) perceived rhythm (all four combined into a "sense of rhythm")

The first two aspects he considers innate forces belonging to earth and man; the third aspect as being acquired or achieved by man. In order to attain a "sense of rhythm" or inner rhythm, he believes there must be awareness of the presence of cosmic and biologic rhythms, and a functioning *with* them in motor performance expression. Having sensory awareness of self and his relationship to the environment allows better performance perception and efficiency so that he is able to move with ease, changing direction of thought and action with measured economy as needed; and perceiving a number of routes or solutions to reach a determined goal.

Having ease and grace in one's performance is being articulate and flexible in language expression as well as in movement; having discrimination in the choice of words; being able to think on one's feet; having imagination. This requires daily practice, not only in "feeling" the beat but in phrasing it with language and movement expression.

What is the difference between beat and rhythm?

"Beat" in music is a repeating pulsation that is a vertical element that can be a regressive force if it is not phrased into linear flow with rhythm. Language, melody and movement make that phrasing.

"Keeping the beat is so often confused with rhythm that the basic function of pulsation is overlooked. Rhythm is what permeates the entire fabric of music; it magnetizes all the musical elements, drawing them together into a vibrating, breathing whole which occupies a specific length of time. Without rhythmic unity there can be no ensemble." [2]

"A most important aspect of rhythm is *flexibility* and not metronomic "time," although this may be one of its functions. Consider that the metronomic beat can be ascribed

to: ♪ ♩ ♩. ♩ ♩. etc. and each can be used for the basic pulse to almost any tempo indication.

It is important to free oneself from a rigid dependence on the quarter note as a basic pulse." [2]

Edgar Juarez, a pioneer of the "new" sound, speaks of rhythm as being and giving the element of stability in the world.

In personal experience I find rhythm to be a self-energizing factor. Moving and speaking *with* the rhythmic flow is never tiring. It is exhilarating, whereas arhythmic (meaning unrhythmic) expression, i.e. halting, jerking or interrupting the natural flow of rhythm, brings a clumsiness and is physically exhausting.

Although rhythm usually contains an underlying heart beat or pulse, if that beat is too heavy or prominent, the rhythmic and/or melodic flow is disturbed, even lost. In

---

[1] "Achieving Perceptual and Motor Efficiency," Vol. I by Ray Barsch (See Bibliography).
[2] Taken from Lecture notes in a course given by Dr. Herbert Zipper.

rock music, for example, the more sophisticated it becomes, the less evident is the underlying beat.

Environment

Rhythm usually permeates a child's expressions. He reinforces his message with muscular action. By nature he speaks or sings *and* moves. Yet today's environment of smog, concrete, violence, and TV, has become alien to his true nature and his needs. Consider the several thousand hours of immobility, lost play and interaction of the present day five-year-old that is taken up by TV watching (18,000 hours for the eighteen-year-old). To compensate, in the classroom we must join movement with learning (rhythmic, expressive, imagery, interaction).

Few children are playing marbles or jacks today. Their small muscles are inactive. Coordination patterns *with* speech and song are needed (clap/snap/patschen, etc.); manipulation with the mallet instruments; transfer of word rhythms on hand drums. Too many children are bored and inactive,[3] both in and outside of school today, yet there is so much more to learn about themselves[4] and their environment, so many more sounds, colors, pictures and worlds to explore.

Answers may lie within *their own* nature and needs: involvement of body, mind and feelings (with nature, fantasy and music); rhythmic expression with hands, feet, voice, and instruments; relationships and relevance to their interests and needs from a starting point of immediacy of needs—doing, finding, relating.

A child does not grow one leg at a time. "All of me grows," explained a four-year old. His statement describes the intent of this approach—a total functioning of the participant, a melding of the feelings and intellect,[5] the affective with the cognitive; language with muscular-motor in a purposeful self-activating expression.

Unfortunately reading or talking about such a philosophy holds little meaning for the newcomer, regardless of his degrees. Understanding seeps in through involvement *with* the process, and the process is the *act* of combining mental and physical faculties and using the subconscious and conscious mind simultaneously.

How does the subconscious function with the conscious mind?

In play the child is close to his subconscious. This area of the brain carries out his repeating patterns (ostinati) after they have been recorded, which frees him to perform the longer text, verse after verse, *and* listen consciously to the total with keen enjoyment. The subconscious is the repeating part of the brain. It plays the "slave"[6] role, doing nothing of its own, merely repeating whatever has been recorded by the conscious mind. This includes a continuous playback of his self image. To erase recorded indentations such as "failure" requires repeated success experiences like those which the child makes for himself in play.

In observing the recording process of a play pattern, I find the sound and the actions being brought together and stabilized by the rhythmic element. The conscious mind listens and feels, recording the performance with a number of repetitions. The appeal

---

[3] According to medical research, the bored, inactive child has less immunity to disease. *Biological Rhythms in Human and Animal Physiology,* by Gay Gaer Luce (Dover Press)

[4] Transactional Analysis: *I'm Okay, Your Okay,* by Thomas A. Harris, M.D. (Harper and Row)

[5] Confluent Education: Human Teaching for Human Learning, by George I. Brown

[6] *Your Child Is Dying To Learn,* by R.R. Gariepy (Barre, Publisher) (See Bibliography)

of the rhythmic content implements the recording process so that the slave mind can soon take over.

After the use of their subconscious is explained to children, they put it to use in muscular patterns with language rhymes, number sequences and ostinato playing on the instruments. They soon find out how necessary it is to *think* the process in order to record it.

Specifics and boundaries

Specifics and boundaries are essential for the well-being of the young student. Lack of specifics [7] often causes the learner to flounder and withdraw. Lack of boundaries often takes away his willingness to explore, and lessens his security. In play the youngster sees specifics and boundaries that he imposes on himself in solving his problems. Whether it concerns space, time, motor or language, he sets boundaries and rules and then proceeds to explore and test the possibilities. His natural affinity for nature and the cosmos rhythms may be related to their specifics in repetition, and in their dependable boundaries. His delight in nonsense verses—when he becomes aware of the difference between sense and nonsense—is another example of his need for specifics. The sense of knowing and knowing that he knows gives him a new worthiness.

Repetition and creativity, as well as specifics and boundaries, are introduced in the 5-tone pentatonic scales with voice and instruments, in language and movement through relationships, differences and likenesses, in space, time and quality. From expressing opposites (up, down; out, in, etc.) to combining and relating different sound textures, rhythms, word phrase and movements, the process can contribute to the development of peripheral sensory functioning as well as learning receptivity and achievement.

Sensory

What is meant by peripheral vision, sight, taste, etc.? Periphery [8] is (a) the outermost part or region within a precise boundary; (b) the region or area beyond a precise boundary; (c) a zone constituting an imprecise boundary. For example, when you focus on a speaker at the front of the room, how much of the room beyond and around the speaker does your vision encompass? Besides the speaker's voice, how much do you hear? of outside sounds? sounds in the room? continuous sounds? unintentional sounds? Staring fixedly at the speaker can soon bring a headache and confusion in one's comprehension. On the other hand, being able to see the speaker in relation to the rest of the room and take in other objects, colors and textures as well, allows clearer reception and understanding of his message. Peripheral vision helps listening comprehension. Peripheral hearing nourishes all the senses.

Why is peripheral sensory functioning important? A great deal has been written about multi-sensory intake and output, and for many years this capability of children has been recognized, yet little has been said or done about developing peripheral sensory functioning and this is really the key to total awareness.

Deliberate and continuing practice in peripheral hearing is an integral part of this approach from the start. First recognizing, and then bringing together in performance two contrasting sound textures, two movements, can greatly enhance the growth of sensory

---

[7] *Failures in Primary Grades,* by Siegfried Englemann. (See Bibliography)

[8] American Heritage Dictionary.

acuity. Awareness of his expanding achievements improves the child's self image and increases his efforts. Working in tonal sound textures and registers heightens and brightens all five senses. In this respect, music can enrich human development a hundredfold.

Movement

One of the primary media of this process which is essential to the child's growth, is *movement*—finding out how he moves, what he moves and where he moves, first in his own sphere (the place in which he stands) and then taking his space to a new place. Again he needs specifics and boundaries to find out about his relationship to the environment, to develop spatial awareness, ease and grace, economy of motion. Laban's science of movement contains these specifics and is the basis for *Verses and Movement* games for children [9].

Leading the entire movement with one part of the body, usually a small muscle, (hand, nose, elbow, etc.), gives a specific focus to the movement. When the child uses opposites in *time* (fast-slow), *weight* (heavy-light), *space* (out-in, up-down, around, etc.) and *space-flow* (linear concept), the movements are brought together with language imagery and problem-solving games *without* any adult example [9]. It is a development of personality in movement by *self-direction*.

Instruments

The child is an instrument of vast scope in sound possibilities—mouth, hands, feet and torso. When he makes contact with other objects or instruments his realm of sounds is unbounded. From birth he is making music, with his hands and feet, gurgling and cooing mouth sounds, imitating and exploring, interpreting and responding to music. His voice, a primary media of communication, is a growing muscle. Two areas of the brain are involved in voice focus—one for singing, one for speaking. (See Chapter on *The Singing Voice.*) Starting with two and three tones, So-Mi-La, which are his from birth, he has specific hand signs, which aid his focus of pitch, and many rhymes to sing. He makes his own chant-like tunes on these three tones, adding his accompaniments with clapping and tonebar instruments; he builds ensembles and organizes musical forms before he reads or writes the symbols.

The hand signs for each tone of the scale come from the work done by the late Zoltan Kodaly of Hungary. They are a significant tool for pitch placement; the child can "see" and manipulate or direct his voice; he can understand tonal space relationships in intervals; he can remember melody easier, and improvise knowledgeably.

The syllables, Do, Re, Mi, Fa, Sol, La, Ti, Do (of Italian origin, and musical in sound) were and are still used in European countries to represent fixed "Do," "C," in pitch. In the American adaptation the Do is movable, according to the key signature and thus may be any given letter. Kodaly combined this use of "movable Do" with hand signs found in an English text (circa 1860) into a game-like approach to knowledgeable singing. A further American translation is herein suggested in this approach in the spelling of the syllables, as follows:

Do, Ray, Me, Fa, So, La, Tee, Do

[9] *Verses and Movement* by G.C. Nash (Music With Children Series.)

It should be noted however, that the child's scale begins on So* rather than Do and therefore his songs will neither begin nor end on Do until he "feels" tonality with the forced resolutions of Tee to Do which occur in the major diatonic or Do scale. If he is "trained" or structured into a "Do" tonality before he has time to explore and make music in his own idiom and scale (pentatonic), there is a gap in his development that makes for rigidity. The difference between *training* and *education,* two words that are antonyms, is shown in this example. In the ensemble building, the voice, singing or speaking, is usually the lead solo part; the other instruments, hand and body percussion or tonebar (glockenspiels, xylophones, timpani, etc.), are the accompaniments and the improvisers of interludes, introductions and endings. The players *are* the singers, the singers *are* the dancers; they bring together a dual performance with the child which is the crux of his development—the process which opens learning receptivity. The rhythmic and melodic elements of the tonebar instruments have a self-stretching appeal and

> He who plays doth also sing,
> or someone else will get your thing!

is the oft-repeated policy verse in this approach.

Tonebar instruments

Specially designed instruments with removable tonebars (see chapter on *Instruments.*) which can be easily played, that have true-tone tuning and encompass different textures (wood, metal, membrane, etc.) and registers of sound, add a dimension to each area of the individual development. Because they are irresistible to the students and offer opportunity for aesthetic experiences; because with careful guidance they bring music making of high quality within reach of every participant; because they bring a success experience and raise self image; their value as instructional materials can hardly be overestimated. They are indispensable to this philosophy.

Pentatonic scales

Important to the success experience with the tonebar instruments and singing is the choice of a scale which is workable for the beginning student. Pentatonic (5-tone) scales which contain no half steps (DO, RAY, ME, SO, LA) are not only natural for the singing voice but also offer and encourage development of performance skills, exploration and experience with early musical forms (canon, rondo, etc.), improvisation and listening acuity.

Why the pentatonic scale?

1) Without a leading tone (the 7th tone is removed) which forces a resolution to Do tonality; without the fourth tone, which has magnetic pull downwards to Me (the third tone), the pentatonic scale becomes a "floating scale." The player is not pulled into a Do ending of his melody. As in his play, he can start and stop at any point and return to it later. The sound will still be consonant. (Halfsteps of the diatonic scale would cause friction when struck simultaneously and the young child would withdraw.)

2) Everyone can play together and be able to hear his own part in relation to the other parts. This is essential in development of peripheral hearing.

3) Each one can improvise his own melody while the others accompany with soft ostinati.

* See page 48 and 53

4) Pentatonic scales are the pillars for all western scales and thereby prepare the student for better understanding of other scales (Diatonic, Modes, Whole Tone, Tonal Row, etc.).

A chart showing the five Pentatonic Scales that can be made on the Diatonic Tonebar instruments can be used by First Level students as well as the Upper Level ones. As an important part of the learning-manipulation, players should set up their own scales.

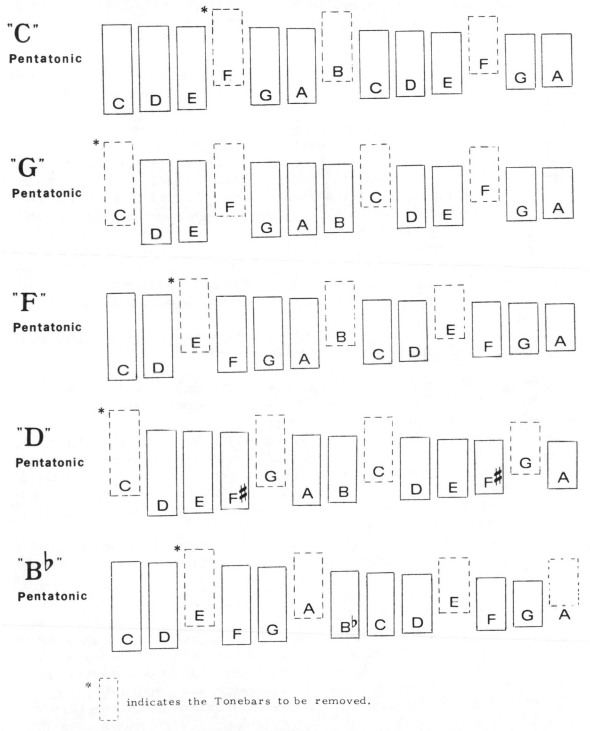

Ostinati patterns can be written on large cards for selection by the players. This short staff-written pattern is an excellent sightreading tool. Accountability and self correction of mistakes are here and now. The student hears what he plays, makes necessary corrections and balances his part with the ensemble. He has to listen attentively in order to fit his part into the total. His concentration must not waver, especially when he is both singing and playing. It could be called "elemental chamber music." This kind of experience triples his rate of progress when he takes up an art form instrument.

The ensemble starts with one instrument and builds one at a time, each added player synchronizing with the others until all are playing together—not the same parts, but each instrument having its individual sound and substance.

The players soon see the advantages in removing the half steps; in fact they often remove any tonebars not being used in order to facilitate their playing precision.

Variations in the ostinati will sometimes allow for a diatonic sequence containing one half step while the other instruments remain in the pentatonic scale; or a song with passing notes that are half steps may have all pentatonic accompaniment.

Premodes in the Pentatonic with "La" or "Ray" as home base for the fifths (borduns) instead of "Do" lead easily into Diatonic Modes, the Major Diatonic and later, the Minors.

The Jazz scale with lowered 7th is an even more natural scale for the American child than the Major Diatonic because it is part of his heritage, expressed in language inflection, as is the syncopated rhythm.

The instruments have a wide scope in the interpretation of poetry, translation of language and movement into sound media and vice versa; translation of word rhythms into melody line; sound scapes and collages that have to do with sound textures in time duration rather than in rhythmic framework; and tonal conversations between two instruments.

Success factors with this prescribed instrumental ensemble are quite dependent on certain uniformities in the construction of the instruments:

1) that all of the tonebar instruments begin with C bar regardless of register.

2) that the tonebars of the different instruments correspond in width so that performance skills easily transfer from one to the other.

3) that the instruments are precision tuned in the true-tone scale rather than a tempered scale of the piano keyboard. (See explanation in chapter on *Instruments.*)

4) that the tonal instruments will encompass four to five different textures and registers: *wood:* xylophones (bass, alto, soprano); *metal:* glockenspiels (alto and soprano); *metal alloy* (aluminum): alto metallophone); *strings:* Guitar; *membrane:* tuned timpani (plastic heads are now used instead of skin).

5) that the first experience of the student be with diatonic instruments which have the extra F♯ and B♭(A♯) tonebars), rather than chromatic instruments. (See *Selection of Tonebar Instruments.*)

Jazz scale

To find the rhythms of a culture, look at the language of that culture. Syncopation and the inflected tones of the lowered 7th and 3rd in American jazz have their origin in our language expression. It is natural for the singing voice. It encompasses improvisation. These are two important considerations for musical exploration and growth.

As stated earlier, the first interval sung by the child is a minor third: So-Me, (Yoo-hoo).

This same interval occurs with the lowered 7th down to the 5th: Tā (or Teh)-So, (Yoo-hoo). Also easy to sing is the half step of lowered 7 to 6, Tā (or Teh)-La.

Such a half step is more natural to sing than either of the half steps in the Major diatonic scale, Fa-Me; Tee-Do, because the lowered 7th does not contain a forced tonality resolution. This half step is more like a voice inflection, a sigh or a feeling of deep emotion. This natural inflection adds a linear flow to the melody and makes improvisation more natural to the singer and player. This lowered 7th added to the pentatonic scale leads the performer into syncopation with the rhythm that is already present in so many spoken words (October, bananas, tacos, Pacific, sister, occur, etc.). Another interesting thing about the half step of the lowered 7th is that many players can improvise together; many singers, also, without frictional sound of dissonance. The melodic line becomes more linear and flowing with the lowered 7th.

EXAMPLE:

From a C pentatonic scale (see chart), go into the jazz idiom by adding tonebar B♭(A♯): C D E — G A B♭ C D E — G A

Using a familiar pentatonic or even So-Me song like *Stop, Look and Listen* (*Today With Music,* Book I), the players begin their familiar ostinati; one player begins to improvise using the new tone B♭ in his melody. Encourage syncopation.

The new sound will be exciting. Gradually other players leave their ostinati patterns and join the improvisations. Urge them to syncopate the rhythms by using word series such as, "September, October, November, December." When a second team of players takes over, the first team tries vocal improvisation, using the song text in any way they wish, as a springboard to their own text recitative style with interaction greetings and conversations as they walk around the room meeting each other. They will be creating their own "West Side Story" or "Porgy and Bess" recitative styles which can lead into mini-operas and music-dramas.

A lowered seventh tonebar can be added to three of the pentatonic scales with the diatonic instruments, before chromatic sets are added:

C Pentatonic, add B♭; G pentatonic, add F; D pentatonic, add C

The lowered 3rd can wait until chromatic sets are added or it can be introduced with two of the pentatonic scales: G, add B♭; D, add F.

Rock style

Rock music can also be handled on the instruments, from a basic hard rock beat against improvised pentatonic melody or a similar ostinato against a diatonic melody played in parallel thirds.

EXAMPLE: Rock ostinato

An ostinato in *moving fifths* in Dorian Mode (Ray scale, See Modes below) with improvisations in Ray diatonic scale brings awareness that rock music has its source in the Dorian Mode.

EXAMPLE:

Harmonic progressions in fifths rather than triads can be practiced in different combinations, such as: I (4 measures), IV (4 measures), I (4 measures), V (2 measures), IV (2 measures), I (2 measures):

I—II—I; II—I—II; V—VI—V, etc.

Diatonic modes

Exploring and understanding the diatonic Modes are important to the understanding of today's music, as well as the historical development of music. These Modes can be easily understood by the facts:

that each Mode has a different starting point or syllable such as, Do to Do or Ray to Ray; that Me and Fah, and Tee and Do are always the half steps wherever they may occur.

Hand signs and movable Do syllables bring to life a clear picture and sound relationship of each Mode as to the location of the half steps. Sing the different Modes with hand signs and from a designated pitch.

EXAMPLES:

Ionian Mode (a Do scale, Major Diatonic) Do, Ray, Me, Fa, So, La, Tee, Do'

Dorian Mode (a Ray scale) Ray, Me, Fa, So, La, Tee, Do', Ray'

Phrygian Mode (a Me scale) Me, Fa, So, La, Tee, Do', Ray', Me'

Lydian Mode (a Fa scale) Fa, So, La, Tee, Do', Ray', Me', Fa'

Mixo-Lydian Mode (a So scale) So, La, Tee, Do', Ray', Me', Fa', So'

Aeolian (a La, natural minor scale) La, Tee, Do', Ray', Me', Fa', So', La'

Lochrian (a Tee scale)

(Notice the marking of half steps: ∨)

On the diatonic instruments the Modes can be introduced and explored from C Major scale which is Ionian Mode. Use Do and So (C and G) fifths for the accompanying ostinato played softly on the instruments, while one player improvises. For Dorian Mode remove the Low C tonebar to clarify the starting tone or home base, Ray=D, in this Mode. (Leave the upper C tonebar on the instruments). Against an ostinato pattern of fifths players

take turns improvising in Dorian Mode. (The same ostinato fifths can accompany singing improvisations.) Pass the melody around until all have tried Dorian Mode. Continue to Phrygian Mode, removing low C and D to show the new starting point, Me. Adding the fifth tone to E (B), design a different rhythmic pattern for the ostinato such as

Moving parallel fifths enhance the accompaniment and challenge the soloist.

EXAMPLE:

*The song, "What Shall We Do With A Drunken Sailor" is in the Dorian Mode. What are the parallel fifths in the accompaniment? And their sequence?

Whole tone scale

Whole tone sequences can be introduced with the diatonic instruments in sound collages before chromatic attachments are made:

C D E F♯ —— B♭ C D E F♯

Taken out of a rhythmic framework, the whole tone scale becomes impressionistic in style; spatial time duration is used rather than beat and rhythm. Developing a picture story in sound, describing feelings, these diffused sound textures offer new possibilities for exploration in poetry and mixed media in colors, movement, language and sound textures—all brought together. Hand percussion, (cymbals, guiro, maracas, triangle, etc.) should be combined with the instruments.

After building an example with the class, have them break into smaller groups with each group selecting an idea, poem, painting or story-experience to portray in sound media.

Harmonic structure

When is a student ready for harmonic structure? Readiness for chord change manipulation can be determined easily through a familiar song that has a I-V-I structure. "Rock-a-my Soul" or "He's Got The Whole World."

* Sing "Row, Row, Row Your Boat" in different
Modes. For example, a Ray scale (Dorian):

R   R | R M F | F M F S etc.

1) Decide on two levels of hand sound such as clapping in front and snapping overhead, for the chord changes. Sing the song *a capella,* using the clapped beat for I, the overhead snap beat for V. (Observing the singers, you can see how many are ready to deal with chord changes on the instruments. Have the others continue to find the chord changes [inner hearing] with the hand sound levels.)

2) At the instruments, use only fifths (boundaries of the triad rather than the three tones). In this way the voice leads and the harmonic changes can be heard more clearly (inner hearing) to direct the mallets.

3) Select a new team of players. (Be sure that the players also sing the song.)

4) Problem Game: To make the I-V-I changes by moving only one mallet instead of the root position change. (There will be a number of solutions.)

5 and 6) Exchange players and try the other song, "He's Got The Whole World." Then combine the two songs, dividing the class.

The next progression I-IV-I can be explored in root fifths; then with one mallet, change:

Try I-IV-V, three chord changes, first with three-hand levels such as patschen, clap and snap with familiar songs ("Jingle Bells," "Silent Night," "Flow Gently Sweet Afton," "Little Brown Church").

Parallel fifths in the song, "Summer Is A-Cumen In" (I-II-I-II)

Triads can be played on the instruments with three mallets. However, too many thirds and sixths will destroy the open beauty of sound that is intended for the instruments, just

14

as too many thirds and sixths in formula music cheapen the sound, thickening it to nausea proportions.

Art form music

Art form classics, chamber music examples and small pieces can be played on the instruments with beautiful results and allow students to taste quality performance long before they are technically proficient on art form instruments to play chamber music. (See book, *Chamber Music for Tonebar Instruments and Recorder,* by Grace C. Nash.) The importance of performing chamber music in small groups using these instruments is dual-purposed: to have the first experience one of an accurately pitched hearing and doing (this gives the student the criteria for judging his later performance with an art form instrument.) and to be able to "get into" the literature, tasting excellence, at an earlier stage of development.

Electronic music

Electronic space music can be simulated with the instruments with various playing techniques to produce tremolos, moving figurations, fluttering sound, glissandos, tone clusters, etc. by using several mallets; a tonebar to produce tone clusters (metal bar on glocks and metallophones, a claves to play xylos). Try stick ends of mallets for glissandos. Rapid finger tremolos with the mallets can be practiced. Combine these with continuous sound produced by rubbing the rims of two or three glass goblets containing water, and shimmering cymbal with finger nails instead of mallet; finger nails rubbing on drum head of the hand drums or brushes used on the hand drums are effective. Add a continuing low human sound or Alto Recorder tone to the total. Compositions titled, Heat, Outer Space, Under the Sea, Antarctica, Atlantis, etc. can be developed.

Music of other cultures

Music of different cultures can be introduced through number sequences with different accents, in 5's, 6's, 7's, 8's, . . . 12's. (See *Rhythmic Coordination* Chapter.) Exposure to different rhythmic sets improves flexibility and brings about sophistication in rhythmic expression. Again, the rhythmic patterns of each culture stem from that particular language. Corresponding movements or folk dances should be added.

"Crossing over the bar" in musical phrases can and should be experienced. Much of contemporary music omits measure bars, or uses them as phrase markings. Latin American rhythms bring sophisticated experience in their changing accents, syncopated and over-the-bar phrases.

Consider the rhythm in the spoken phrase, "Latin American tune> >" This is an example of the Bossa Nova pattern, 8 - 4 in an over-the-bar phrase. This pattern has been called

"universal rhythm" [10] with its three beats in 8-8ths instead of the usual four beats, followed by a rest and two quarter beat accents and a rest. Sophisticated in its content, it is a freeing kind of expression which brings flexibility and sense of rhythm to the performer. The Bossa Nova can be performed with patschen; do the accents with one hand on one knee, the other numbers with the other hand and knee.

[10] *Book of Today's Drumming,* by Norman Grossman New York: Amsco, 1971 (See Bibliography)

EXAMPLE:

Patschen R.

L.

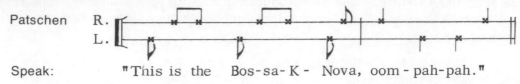

Speak: "This is the Bos-sa-K- Nova, oom - pah-pah."

Transferring this kind of rhythmic sophistication to nursery rhymes and sayings, exploring the possibilities out of the original or given rhyme, open many avenues for experimentation that are within reach of the young student (upper elementary and middle school). Moving over the accent in a 4-meter saying, for example, lengthens the meter:

(Clap the accents; walk the words.)

"First come, first served, First come, first served, First come, first served," etc.

PETER, PETER, PUMPKIN EATER

Pet - er was known as a pump - kin eat - er And
he had a wife and he could not keep her So

he put her in - to a pump - kin shell and there

he kept her, he kept her ver - y, ver-y well in-deed, in-deed.

Notation

Notation is an intellectual statement of the experience. Where language is expressed and used long before the child reads and writes it, the same principle can apply to notation in music. Expressing rhythm and melody in many ways (speaking, moving, playing) prepares him for the abstract symbols. Physical manipulation of symbols in the form of rhythm sticks, popsicle sticks or mallets, cuisenaire rods, also clarify written symbols.

Hand signs are also a muscular manipulation that is invaluable in making the transition to notation symbols. All of these can be introduced quite early as readiness games. These rhythmic symbols have their source in the work done by Zoltan Kodaly and are basic to all traditional notation:

RHYTHMIC NOTATION

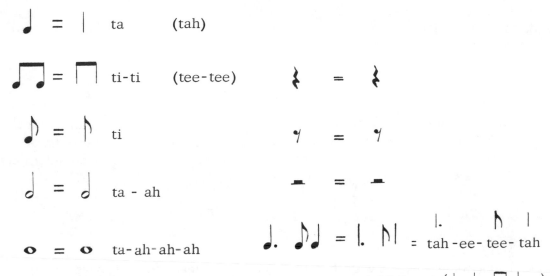

Rearrangements and extensions of the primary rhythm of childhood (| | ⊓ |) .

"One, Two, tie my shoe" are made by the students in a Stick-Roof game: | | ⊓ |

Question: Where else can the roof stick be placed? What is the new pattern?"

| ⊓ | | etc.

Transferring these patterns to the chalk board produces a longer reading line that can be performed in many ways: clapped forwards, then backwards; spoken and clapped with tah's and ti's; played on different hand percussion instruments; an ostinato added and played on two timpani drums; sung on So and Me, alternating measures, etc.

REST GAME | | | ⁊
    A quarter rest (⁊) game stemming from the verse, "Ding, Dong, Bell."

Question: Where else could the rest be placed?

| ⁊ | | , ⁊ | | | , | | ⁊ | . . .

Exploring possibilities brings a longer line to perform in various ways like the above.

THE FLOATING ROOF GAME
    Line up five sticks on the floor: | | | | |

An extra stick is offered to the volunteer who will make a new pattern by placing a roof over two of the walls (sticks). The different possibilities make for a continuing line to remember each addition (no writing on the board), or a written transfer of each pattern to extend the reading line.

Introducing staff reading [11] can begin with two lines for hand sounds: right and left hand claps; two levels of clap and patsch (leg pat) transferred to two percussion instruments; two pitches, So and Me.

With pitch reading, the advice is to *make haste slowly.* Producing pitch with an instrument or voice requires psychological organization. It should be presented first in comfortable pulse framework, later in a rhythmic setting. Lines and spaces are added according to the voice development in reading. Here again, hand signs, syllables and the tonebar instruments are invaluable tools for precision and placement of pitch on the staff.

NEW NOTATION

Interpretation of new notation by the students, in movement, mouth sounds and with instruments, extends their imagination and abilities, awareness and interest-efforts. For example, with three teams: movement, mouth sounds and instruments, ask for interpretation of the following example:

Which media communicates with the most impact? the least Impact? Which media are the most difficult to use? (Instruments) Can two groups be combined in their performance?

New notation designed by the students can begin on large wrapping paper as a team project; a story composition; abstract or impressionistic, according to their decisions. Each composition is performed for the class. Exchanging manuscripts gives each team an idea of the clarity of their notation symbols, which is an important factor in the purpose and use of notation.

In total, consider these findings with respect to the role of sound textures (instruments) in this approach to child development:

1) Sound, especially rhythmic sound, focuses attention of eye, ear and motor, according to Ray Barsch*. How quickly a rhythmic pattern, clapping, a drum, Morse code or bugle ignites the attention, even in a conversation-filled room. Such a pattern instinctively calls for a repetition of the pattern (echo) or an answer phrase; and even though the reply may not be given, the human desire for it is still there. This provides a natural key to focusing and activating mental and physical faculties. Use language, muscular and motor together, in rhythmic expression.

2) Dealing with pitch, loudness and timbres (textures) requires psychological organization.* To produce pitch or melody with the voice or other instruments, the performer has to think, organize and listen. To fit a pattern (ostinato) into the larger ensemble of instruments, one must hear relationships and be concerned with balance in the total sound. This places a self-stretching, high demand on the participants.

3) Tonal sound arrests all human response and affects all five senses. How many times each school day the class bell breaks into the student's thoughts, stopping all

[11] See *Today With Music, Book I*
Achieving Perceptual and Motor Efficiency, Vol. I by Ray Barsch

sensory intake and response. A single bell sound will cause an infant of one month to cease his activity, according to Gesell (1939).

With the continuous sound in our environment, silence is only relative. The ways in which sound and tonal sound can affect all five senses are of concern in this approach, as follows: (a) a heavy bombardment of sound will block out all sensory intake, not only hearing. If the bombardment lasts too long, there is damage to the hearing sense. Auditory impairment causes imbalance in the other senses. (b) a continuous sound or conglomerate of sound, such as Muzak or a continuing drip-drop of water without inflection, will dull the senses. It is a sedative to the mind. (c) a selective involvement with contrasting sound textures and registers will heighten sensory acuity. The earlier that tonal sound is brought into the child's awareness translating his environment such as wind, rain, bird songs, etc. into tonal textures, the more totally aware he becomes to his environment. Tonal sound offers a direct path to total awareness.

4) The newborn infant recognizes his mother's voice within a few hours after birth, with a response of wellbeing in the form of opening movements of his hands and body (harsh, raucous sounds will cause him to recoil and tighten). That rhythm and melody are innate forces at birth, places them at the core of human expression and development. Their expression should begin with the lullabies and rhymes and with the mother's swaying motions as she holds the infant. Chanting of the three tones should be encouraged from infancy and at school, combined with rhythmic patterns in the hands and feet.

CONCLUSIONS

In my observation of students who are involved in this kind of total learning based on this philosophy, I am quite sure they are using more than five percent of their brain cells. Their self-stretching, rapid performance-growth is far beyond the usual traditional standards. Evidence of their high level of interest and effort is shown in their eyes, in the fact that they do not waste time but prefer to "get on" with the project at hand. They want greater degrees of excellence in the outcome and they are able and eager to work together, rather than separately, to produce a better result. Cooperation—contribution—listening—concentration—"try it again"—Ahhhhhh!

This philosophy acknowledges that:

1) Music encompasses more disciplines than are possible in any single subject.

2) Language plays the role of the development of intelligence; that it clarifies any rhythmic problem. (Lack of language often causes violence.)

3) Sound makes the first track to the brain, and movement is the infant's first response to sound. Movement is a necessity of life. Lack of movement can cause mental retardation.

4) The ear is the most flexible organ of the human body; after hearing a sound three times, the brain accepts it as valid! [12]

5) Rhythm and melody are innate forces from birth and therefore need to be expressed and sophisticated if the person is to become a complete adult.

6) Without the expressive and creative arts, man cannot survive; his existence would become ape-like. (Reported from a conversation with anthropologist E.A. Hoebel.)

[12] from Lecture Notes by Dr. Herbert Zipper

7) Change has become an elemental force requiring greater flexibility in the human being. To have flexibility he must also have stability. The arts are the stabilizers needed for human survival.

SUMMARY

This philosophy brings together
- the graphic notation symbols, and the so-fa syllables with hand signs as developed by Zoltan Kodaly of Hungary
- the instruments and sound textures, heritage rhymes and elemental music as unfolded by Carl Orff and Gunild Keetmann of Germany
- the principles of movement as designed by Rudolf Laban and his exponents in England

into a composite philosophy that is right for American children in their constantly changing environment.

It is a media process that is open-ended, a working philosophy that proves itself in the *doing.*

The techniques are basic to the child, to all musical performance, to language expression, and to movement coordination and flow.

The ingredients or media are drawn from the environment and language, human qualities and experiences of the participants.

The process is problem-solving, and the extensions peripheral.

It is directed to serve the student—to:

F̲OCUS attention into alertness and aliveness.

E̲NGAGE mental and physical faculties.

E̲XPAND awareness into peripheral sensory functioning.

D̲EVELOP skills and flexibility.

the total child toward more able, joyous and self-directing adulthood.

FORMULA

Cn + (r+m)L = GHP

Explanation: Take a given number of Children, (add rhythm and melody-movement) multiply by Learning (or injected in learning) and this brings or equals Greater Human Potential.

CHAPTER 2

Creative Approach to Rhythmic Coordination

Rhythmic experience aids coordination and freedom of expression. Muscular coordination enables the individual to move gracefully and confidently. No longer concerned with or inhibited by clumsiness, he may assume a sense of well being which will enable him to become a more articulate person in music as well as in other media.

Coordination begins with the use of body sounds in rhythmic accompaniment to speech. The hands and feet are translated into instruments of sound which occur in *space* and *time* and have an element of *quality, timbre* or *weight.*

Rhythm is a life force and according to Carl Orff, rhythmic exercise proves beneficial to all children. Dr. R. Van Allen[1] indicates that a child who cannot respond physically to music will probably be too tense and withdrawn to respond to printed symbols. On this basis, would it not be wise to try music and do more music making first or to bring language and rhythmic expression together in music and movement?

This chapter on rhythmic coordination, while involving muscular and motor action, is separated from the chapter on movement because of its specialized focus. In this chapter, we will be dealing with muscular action sounds in rhythmic settings derived from and accompanying speech texts while attempting to use the arms and legs as percussion instruments; expressing and combining rhythmic contents, coordinating two or more action sounds with speech. Both chapters are essential to understanding the development of flexibility and coping with abilities needed to become a more adaptive human being in our rapidly changing society.

A major goal in rhythmic-coordination practice is to reach the stage of being able to *internalize* the beat and the rhythmic line. The preparation for this is *externalizing,* —expressing both with the muscles, body and speech.

A second goal is the utilization of the subconscious in its role of repeating patterns (as muscular sound patterns used in play), and hence to facilitate accomplishment and adaptiveness. To bring this about, students must be made aware of the tremendous force

---

[1]Dr. R. Van Allen—consultant to Project Prolexia—E S S A—Title III, Riverside County, California 92502.

for learning which lies in their subconscious.[2] It is important with each new pattern to establish and consciously record the muscular action, sounds and speech for playback by the subconscious, which frees the conscious mind for other and added parts.

RHYTHMIC COORDINATION

Coordination is the synchronized functioning of muscles or groups of muscles in the execution of a complex task. The task starts quite simply in a framework of rhythmic speech with muscular sounds, for example: space clapping with a heritage rhyme where speech combines with muscular action sounds for maximum development.

Space clapping with heritage rhyme "Pease Porridge Hot"

1) Separate the phrases in the verse by looking to the right and clapping the beat as you speak. When the next phrase starts, look to the left.

R. "Pease	porridge	hot, ‰		L. Pease	porridge	cold,	
R. Pease	porridge	in the pot,		L. nine	days	old. ‰	
R. Some	like it	hot, ‰		L. some	like it	cold, ‰	
R. Some	like it	in the pot,		L. nine	days	old." ‰	

We find there are four claps (beats) in each phrase. This *set* of four beats is the phrase unit with which we have to work.

The simplest outlining of the phrase would be to clap the fourth beat in another place. Where else can you clap other than in front? Many answers suggest themselves: "overhead, behind, to the side, even under the knee." Selecting one of the easiest to do first, we'll do the fourth clap overhead in each set. This plan will carry through the verse like an ostinato. Establish the set *before* adding the verse:

2)   Clap   etc.

2a) With intermediate classes, put it in canon. The second part enters two beats after the first part.

3) Try new space clapping on the fourth beats such as:

- first phrase overhead,

- second phrase behind,

- third phrase to the left side,

- fourth phrase to the right.

[2] See explanation Pg. 37 and 38 in Chapter 4 on Music for Total Learning.

On the second verse, repeat the first two phrases but on the third and fourth phrases, clap under each knee.

4) Clap the words (no speaking) and *snap* the *rests.*

5) *Walk* the four beats to each phrase and say the verse. In limited space walk forward on first phrase, back up on second phrase, etc. Express the rests with elbows "thumping" space.

6) Transfer the words to your feet and clap the rests. To keep from stepping on the rests, balance on one foot, dipping the body and pointing the other foot forward in space. Try other heritage rhymes or sayings with muscular action sounds.

Coordinating large movements with speech text

EXAMPLE:

1) Begin with a slow walk to the words "First come, first served," one step to each word.

2) To the words "keep calm," the arms move in parallel motion, outlining a large figure 8 on its side, swinging downward to the left on "keep," over and downward to the right on "calm."

Walk around the room speaking "keep calm" with the arm motion while thinking (inner hearing): "First come, first served" which is being expressed by the feet.

3) Continue the arm movement and *double* the walking steps to the text.

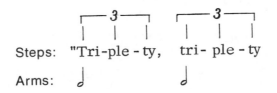

See you la - ter, al - li - ga - tor.

4) After four patterns of the walking pace in #3, return to four patterns of the walking pace in #1. Alternate these two patterns against the same half note swing of the arms until the transitions are smoothly executed.

5) Extend the exercise to a triplet-step pattern which is somewhat slower than the eighth-notes and yet somewhat faster than the quarter notes:

Steps: "Tri-ple - ty, tri- ple - ty

Arms:

Three walking steps to each downward swing of the arms.

6) Variations of the arm motion: Swing arms in opposite directions in the figure 8 pattern.

Clap/Patschen

Patschen is a German word meaning leg-slap. Using right and left legs, right and left hands, there are four different sounds possible.

    1) Use a familiar counting rhyme such as: "One, two, tie my shoe." Clap the numbers, answer with patschen, L. R. L. etc. Continue through to 10. Make up a text for the count-down: "10, 9, hold that line" etc.

    2) Walk the beats: L, R, L, R, L, R etc. and repeat the above in clap and patschen.

    3) Take away the speech except first and last words, "One . . . hen" and do the clap/patschen. Keep the rhythm of text.

    4) Combine feet *walking* the *words* with the clap/patschen and *speaking* the text.

Combining one rhythmic pattern with a contrasting text.

    Clap the pattern: This is the universal rhythmic pattern of childhood. In every culture over the world this rhythmic pattern is found in some sort of counting-out rhyme.

EXAMPLES:

Pop, pop, lollypop,	Stash trash in the sack,
Buy one at the barbershop,	Left and right, front and back;
One for you, one for me,	Bitter litter, hie away,
Out you go on 1, 2, 3!	1, 2, Out! I say.

    1) Try clapping this ostinato while singing a familiar song such as "Frère Jacques" or speaking a familiar verse.

    2) Variations of this exercise can be found in the song materials, such as doing a three beat pattern against a song that is in four meter.

EXAMPLE: Clap partner's right hand with your right hand on 1, partner's left hand with your left hand on 2, clap own hands on 3, while singing or speaking "One, two, tie my shoe." Another three beat pattern is simply: clap, patsch R., patsch L.

Combinations.

    1) The stamp, representing the lowest level in space and the strongest (gravity) in weight, expresses the *accented beat* in this exercise.

EXAMPLE:

Begin with a stamp and 1 clap for several times; stamp and two claps for several times. Alternate the patterns: stamp — clap, stamp — clap — clap, stamp — clap, stamp — clap

— clap; adding the voice counting to 10 and back. Maintain the patterns.

2) Add a third sequence of: stamp — clap — clap — clap, to the above sequence and count by 2's as far as you can go without a mistake. Count backward by 2's from a given number.

3) Try walking in a changing meter, two and three, and accenting *1* in each set as:

ONE - two, ONE - two - three, ONE - two, ONE - two - three, etc. As you walk, clap
> > > >

these accents in a different place in space each time, such as — overhead, side, back, etc.

Four-sound pattern with walking:

Clap, Patschen L., Patschen R., Snap

Establish this pattern, then add walking, one step to each sound.

1) If this is successful, add speaking with a familiar rhyme such as, "One, two, . . ." or "Peter, Peter, pumkin eater" etc.

2) Do this same pattern with a familiar song such as "Three Blind Mice . . ."

Triplets and the beat together

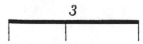

1) Pattern: Clap – Patsch R – Patsch L.   Use this pattern with 3-syllable word series using sports, presidents and/or animals as categories.

EXAMPLE:

Speak — Wash-ing-ton, Jef-fer-son, Roo-se-velt, Ken-ne-dy, etc.

2) Add slow walking step — on first syllable of each word. The step goes with the clap.

"Doublets" and the beat together

1) Pattern: Clap — Patsch R or L. Using 2—syllable names as — Jack-son, Lin-coln,

John-son, etc.

2) Add the same walking beat, stepping with each *clap* on the *first* syllable.

Combining two patterns in a changing meter sequence

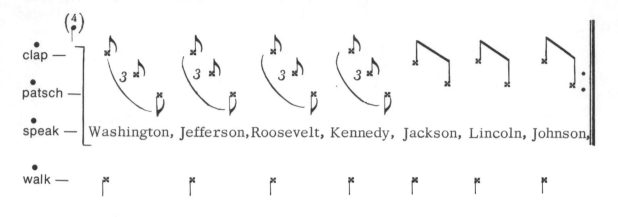

Take away the speech and do the sequence. Notice (a) that the slow walking step requires motor control and a flow or fluid kind of slow motion, and (b) that the beat remains steady throughout.

This combines (slow) motor coordination with a faster muscular coordination; with the objective of developing and maintaining a linear flow throughout.

Beat and after-beat

1) Using the same *2-syllable* word series, separate the two muscular sounds into a *stamp-clap* action.
2) Change the stamp to a walking step and repeat the above.
3) A sequence using beats doubled, tripled in after-beats (two muscular sounds).
Beginning with basic beat in walking: x   x   x   x   etc.

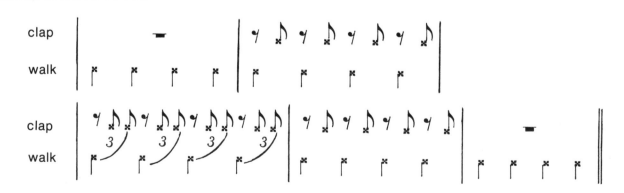

Rhythmic speech Ensemble

Rondo
"I Like Hot Dogs"

Grace C. Nash

(A)

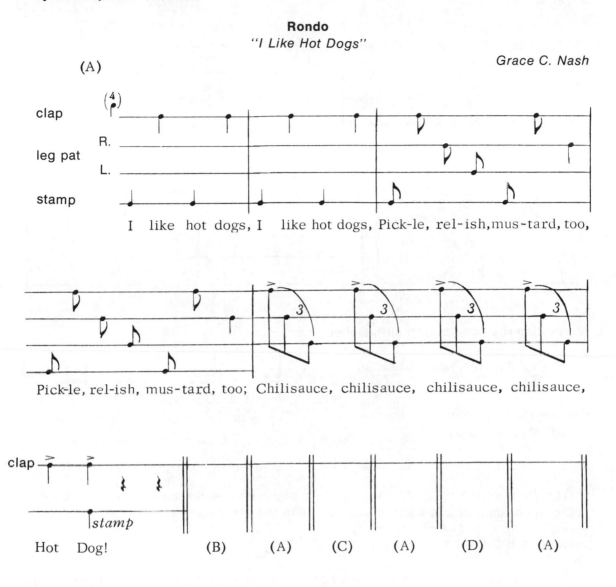

clap

leg pat   R.
         L.

stamp

I   like hot dogs, I   like hot dogs, Pick-le, rel-ish, mus-tard, too,

Pick-le, rel-ish, mus-tard, too; Chilisauce, chilisauce, chilisauce, chilisauce,

clap

stamp

Hot   Dog! (B) (A) (C) (A) (D) (A)

SUGGESTIONS:

1) The above six measures can be the (A) section of Rondo form, to be done by group, and the sections (B), (C), (D) will be improvised Solos. After each improvised Solo, the group repeats (A), six measures, again.

2) In case the 3rd & 4th bars are too difficult for the entire group to do, have only those who are proficient do these two bars. On measures 5 & 6, everyone *claps* the 6 beats while several students do the triplets. In this way precision and clarity of speech and rhythm can be maintained.

27

3) This rhythm can also be transferred to percussion instruments effectively, for example:

Triangle

Wood block

Drum

Tambourine

Alternating rhythmic patterns (Patschen)

1) Patschen the beat on one leg —

Patschen the words on the other —
  2) Reverse the parts.

"See you la - ter, Al-´ li - ga - tor."

NOTE: Some of the difficulty here can be eased with greater space used by the hand doing the beats. Lift this hand into space. Keep the other hand closer to the leg for the

faster speech pattern.

Try this same combination with walking the beat, while clapping the rhythm; exchange parts.

Number sets with accents placed

Beginning with a six beat sequence: 1 2 3 4 5 6

a) *Speak* the numbers and *clap* #1 to the right side; #4 to the left side.

b) Try three accents: #1, 3, 5   1 2 3 4 5 6

c) Two Groups: Group I claps (a) as Group II claps (b). Both groups count the numbers.

Try walking the numbers and clapping the accents.

Accent other numbers.

d) Use a set of eight beats:

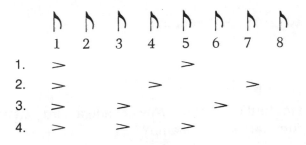

	1	2	3	4	5	6	7	8
1.	>				>			
2.	>			>			>	
3.	>		>			>		
4.	>		>		>			

After trying these different accents, divide into four groups. Add a percussion instrument to each group and set up the ensemble. Add 1 drum and finger cymbals or triangle on a two measure ostinato such as:

Finger Cymbals —

Drum —

VARIATIONS:

1) Perform these sets above with patschen, doing the accented numbers on left leg with left hand and the other numbers on right leg with right hand.

2) Perform the sets on table top using both hands as in #1.

3) Perform the sets on a hand drum held between the knees; on bongo drums or on a floor drum.

Notice how these sets go into Latin American rhythms such as bossa nova, rumba, samba, etc.

Two against three with Patschen

Guidelines 1: Multiply 2 × 3 = 6 ("6" will be the set). With two accents, there will be three numbers to each accent; with three accents, two numbers to each accent.

a) 1   2   3   4   5   6   for the two division
   >   >

b) 1   2   3   4   5   6   for the three division
   >   >   >

Speak and perform (a) with left hand patschen on left leg, and (b) with right hand patschen on right leg.

Start with (b) establishing the muscular action. Add (a), performing both patterns simultaneously.

Guidelines 2: For two different accent groupings against each other, multiply them together to obtain the "set" number. For example, to analyze three against four, the set would be twelve. Divide it into groupings for three accents. 12 ÷ 3 = 4 (4 numbers in each group with the first of each group accented.

a) 1, 2, 3, 4, 5, 6, 7, 8, 9, 10, 11, 12 - 3 accents

b) 1   4   7   10   - 4 accents

Perform (a) with one hand patschen on table top or drum; perform (b) with other hand patschen on table top or drum.

Extension: Try two against five for further practice. Why not add a third part accenting other numbers in the set and perform this with a "stamp?"

Performing three rhythmic lines; coordinating voice, hands and feet

Clap

Speak | Ta- ah, Ta-ah, | Ta-ah, Ta-ah, | Ta - ah, Ta- ah, | Ta-ah, Ta, rest.
Stamp Softly

a) Try only two lines: speak and stamp, then speak and clap.
b) Put all three lines together. (This is difficult!)
c) When this is successful, reverse the two top lines.
1) Try this example:

Speak:

Clap:

Stamp:

Reverse "Speak and Clap" lines above.

Rhythmic Pattern, Stamp / Clap, Against Non-Rhythmic Speech Directions:
    1) Partners Game

    2) Establish a three pattern ostinato: stamp - clap - clap.
    3) Both partners continue this pattern together.
    4) "A" speaks, telling about himself, his after-school activities, as both partners

continue the pattern. "B" replies, telling how his after-school schedule is different.

The idea is not to let the rhythmic pattern waver during the conversation. This may be very difficult at first, but with repeated tries over a period of several weeks, it is achieved and the new freedom/release is exhilarating!

Other games for coordination

1) Clapping a given song in canon with one's singing. Try "Frère Jacques" and begin clapping the song two measures after the singing starts. See page 45 in chapter on "Music for Total Learning." Try "Three Blind Mice," "Swanee River" and other familiar songs this way.

2) Sight-read a rhythmic line, clap it in canon with the ta and ti-ti speaking.
EXAMPLE:

Speak —

Clap —

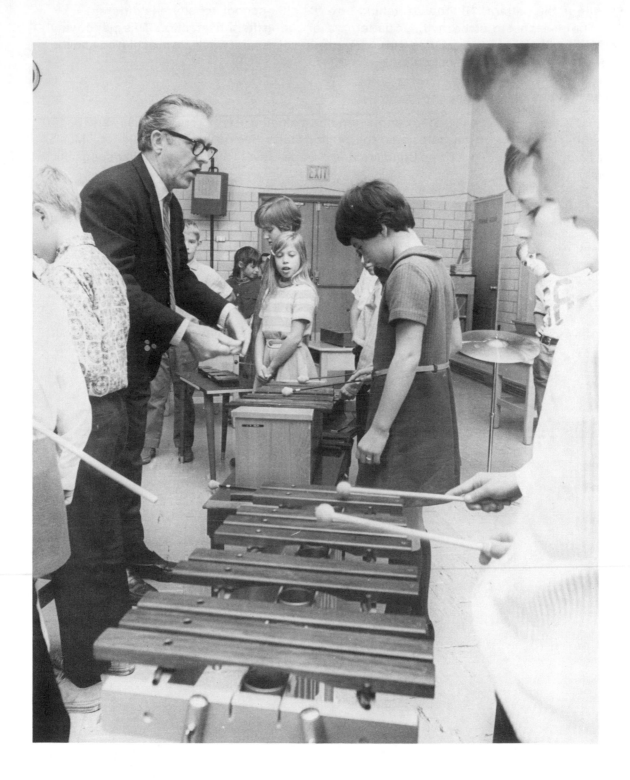

CHAPTER 3

Music for TOTAL Learning and Learning Aids in the Classroom

Exciting alternatives can be found in almost any area of learning today—alternatives that can bring joy into otherwise difficult tasks at school. Music, with its natural appeal, its healing elements and its inherent disciplines, offers all kinds of alternatives and aids to *other* subjects. Its elements of rhythm and melody are vehicles for joyous learning, even total growth of the child.

1) Instead of teaching music as a subject, let's apply music to the problem of *spelling:* the days of the week, for example. Divide the class into two groups. Group I begins with the word *day.*

Clap and spell in rhythm. d-a-y

group II clap & speak
Capital   S-u-n

Group I clap & speak
d-a-y

(Both groups then speak).

Sun-day   Sun-day

Following the same plan for the other days of the week, the rhythms are:

Group II clap
Capital   M-o-n

Group I clap
d-a-y

Monday, Monday

Capital   T-u-e-s

d-a-y

Tuesday, Tuesday

```
┌┐ |  ┌┐ |           ┌┐ |
Capital   W-e-d,  n-e-s       d-a-y

        Wednesday,  Wednesday

        ┌┐ ┌┐ |             ┌┐ |
Capital   T-h-u-r-s          d-a-y
        Thursday,  Thursday

          ┌┐ |               ┌┐ |
Capital    F- r- i           d-a-y

          Friday,  Friday

        ┌┐ |  |  |           ┌┐ |
Capital   S- a- t,  u - r    d-a-y

        Saturday,  Saturday
```

Speak: Days of the week, days of the week . . . Let's spell them again and write them complete.

Group II begins this time, one student at the board writing the "Sun" as they clap and speak. Group I answers "d-a-y" as one student adds these letters to the above. With each succeeding day, two students do the writing of the word.

Later, this episode can be recognized as a Rondo Form, with the "d-a-y" being the repeating "A" Section.

The spelling of the months, such as: September, October, November, December, can be enjoyed and learned much faster when put into rhythmic structure. Out of this comes recognition of form, as well. Soon children can do their own rhythmic patterns out of difficult words . . . exploring possibilities for themselves.

2) Let's try an arithmetic problem (Oral, aural learning).

EXAMPLE: $\textcircled{4} \times 2 + 3 = ?$

Put the <u>4</u> into four beats on a hand drum, or 4 taps on the desk top then speak the other numbers: (drum) $1 - 1 - 1 - 1 \times 2 + 3 = ?$ (11)

The rhythmic beat draws immediate attention and activates listening. Soon two of the numbers can be played on a drum or wood block. Longer attention span and faster thinking-on-the-spot are natural results.

Using the tone call of "yoo-hoo" (So-me), sing problem on the first pitch, (so) awaiting the answer on the lower tone (me).

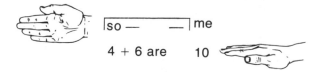

```
        ⌐so —        — ⌐me
        4 + 6 are    10
```

EXAMPLE:

Class answers (sings) on "me" to complete the melody chant.

Here the natural desire for completion of the phrase tune accelerates the thought process.

3) A short time of "singing only" (no speaking) during a class day can be a stirring and thoughtful change of habits. Instructions, questions, requests, answers, conversations are all done with the singing voice; sometimes it may be only one tone, two tones or even three tones.

A good preparation for such a turn of events is the introduction of hand signals for tonal relationships. Beginning with the 2-tone, "yoo-hoo" or "So-me," develop, through games, a secure accuracy of pitch by singing nursery rhymes, sayings and experiences on these two tones according to each child's wishes—his tune—as he leads the class with hand signals. A third tone, "la" completes the universal folk tune of childhood, heard the world around, "I've got a secret."

These muscular signals in space enable children to focus the desired pitch, to manipulate their voices knowledgeably and to sing with self-confidence. And for those who haven't found their singing voices, these hand signals can represent the vocal instrument, which otherwise cannot be seen nor understood. With the hand as the voice and starting with "so" (which is his natural place to start) the child *draws* the wall sign of "so" away from him, as if drawing the tone out of his mouth. It comes! And with each successive try it becomes stronger and more secure. Limiting his singing to two and then three tones in range, but from different starting pitches until his control and hearing are established, is the guideline. In fact this is a guideline to follow for all young children. Giving them songs of too wide a range not only harms their singing voices but forces them to sing by rote, by guess, and by approximation. When will educators consider how important to one's well-being is the ability to sing? Every child who can sing has added one more dimension to his self-expression. And as an adult he can give vent to his loneliness or his exuberance, in company or in solitude.

Returning to this short time of "singing only," the outcomes will be many. Some children will enjoy it thoroughly and ask for longer such periods. Others who "spoke" too often will now sing too seldom. And the shy ones will be at first even more reticent. Yet, a story line that is sung, developed by their contributions, will draw out some of the students, especially when creative dramatization is added. It may even ignite an original mini-drama with improvised solos which further the plot.

Another probable outcome is more musical speech inflection and phrasing, better organization of their thoughts and feelings and certainly a decrease in idle verbiage!

4) When the classroom gets exceedingly noisy, a bid for silence by clapping a rhythmic pattern with an implied text such as:

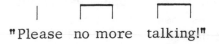

"Please no more talking!"

will get an immediate response—perhaps it will be an implied answer, clapped,

"Yes, thank you, yes."

Let's explore some alternatives in a familiar song.
(On the board:)

1. What song is this? (Each measure is repeated.)
2. Can you clap it? (Each measure is repeated.)
3. Can you sing it on 'loo'' or a neutral syllable? (Who thinks they recognize the tune?) ("Frère Jacques" or "Are You Sleeping?")
4. Select one measure to clap as a repeated pattern throughout the song. Establish the rhythmic pattern before adding the song with words.
5) Can you transfer this pattern to two percussion instruments such as a woodblock and triangle? (Two players who sing while playing.) The rest of the class sings with the players.
6) Can you sing the song as a "round" with *yourself?!*
Clap the 2nd part. Sing the first part.
7) Can you clap the song backwards? This time do not repeat each measure.
8) Choose a partner who will clap it forwards against your clapping it backwards. (Do not repeat any measures.)
9) Who could change the first measure? You may borrow from any of the remaining measures to change it. Follow with 2nd measure; another student (same rules) does the 3rd measure; and 4th measure.
10) Clap the new rhythm. Clap it backwards. Which way sounds better?
11) Can you make a new tune on this rhythm? Use the same scale tones as in "Frère Jacques"—or on three tones only, such as, so, me, la or on five tones, pentatonic scale la, so, me, re, do.

These are only some of the possibilities that lie within one short song. It is easy to see how written notation can evolve from direct experience with rhythmic content of a song. Fluent rhythmic reading carries the flow of pitch reading, and sight reading should evolve in phrase reading rather than in beat-by-beat or note-by-note process.

WHAT IS PLAY?

The answer, translated from writings of J. Huizinga, states that play is a factor of culture. It satisfies ideals of expression and of living together. Play creates order and imposes a limited perfection upon the imperfect world and the confused life. It is recognized that children learn fastest and happiest in their play. To find out more about their nature and their needs, let us observe the ingredients of play. Play involves:

1) repetition, which is necessary to the child's security. Where adult security lies in certainty, children *need* repetition.
2) movement, muscular action—essential to their health and human development.
3) rhythm, the organizer of patterns that are repeated and extended in speech, sound and action. Rhythm is the core of play.

4) language in rhymes, chants and rules. Language is inseparable from thought.

5) use of the subconscious in doing two, three and even four things simultaneously. The subconscious is the "slave" mind. A non-thinking, non-emotional repeating part of the mind which carries out orders given by the conscious mind without the aid or interference from the conscious mind (walking, eating, etc.) Just as it sustains and repeats the self-image, it also generates the complex patterns found in play. When children enter school they are still close to their subconscious. How natural it would be to utilize it in school learning.

Further, play involves:

6) release from or absence of fear and tensions.

7) risks, taken within their own prescribed boundaries and rules.

8) success and/or failure, accepted without pressure or fear from adult worlds.

9) problem solving. Practically all play contains some element of problem solving or investigating, from a team game to studying a green worm under a cabbage leaf. Children are curious and investigative. In play, there is preparation for adult life.

10) humor and nonsense. Nonsense is important to children's well-being, enabling them to discern differences between reality and fantasy, sense and nonsense.

11) flexibility and spontaneity. The rules in play can be and are changed momentarily to fit the players and the situation, without harm to anyone.

ATTITUDES OF CHILDREN

Attitudes of children toward school, their readiness and receptivity quotients, although individually different, may also have certain common denominators. LISTEN to their talk:

"School is for learning . . . I don't want to spend the day playing games or doing baby stuff. Each day I want to feel good about what I have learned in school such as things I didn't know about yesterday."

"I want to feel smart . . . like I can do that, too."

"Teach me . . . show me . . . let me alone. If it's important I'll learn it, but don't waste my time with things and reasons I don't need or care about."

"What are grades? Just letters or numbers that Dad and Mom want to see and talk about. How can one letter or one number mean anything anyway? It takes many letters to make a word. Letters aren't worth much by themselves and numbers aren't either unless they belong to something like apples or birds . . . so why all the fuss?"

PLAY TECHNIQUES IN THE CLASSROOM

How can the ingredients and techniques of play be used in the classroom? Understanding play should enable teachers to utilize these techniques and ingredients in learning situations, to facilitate, even accelerate the learning process and certainly to add a light touch of pleasure to a tedious task.

Consider the formula: "Combine a distasteful task with irresistible media and the result is a palatable task!" EXAMPLE: State an arithmetic or spelling problem with rhythm (drum) and the result is achievement!

Use techniques of play wherever they will help children. Introduce nonsense and laughter, risks and rhymes. Use lots of movement, repetition and rhythm, discovery-problems to ponder, flexibility in rules, and joy. Add challenge that may involve failure as well as success; subtract pressure and fear, tension and labels; delete "don't" and "do's . . . or else" and try not to give answers to questions which children have not yet asked!

Counting games

"Ringo, rango, tingo, tango,
Dinosaurs *in shoes*,
Bingo, bango, lingo, lango,
I can count by *twos* : 2, 4, 6, etc."

Going up in numbers use:
"with knees" . . . . . "threes"
indoors . . . . . fours
alive . . . . . fives
and sticks . . . . . six
in heaven . . . . . sevens
are late . . . . . eights
on time . . . . . nines
again . . . . . tens

The counting can be done by single student or class. Proceed as far as possible without a mistake. This can be a team game also.

Come along Mary, Come along John, Come along Jerry, Come along Don,
Ev'ryone join and count by (2) up to (20) and *back* again
(3) up to (30) and *back* again

In the above example, the subconscious can be harnessed for the replay or countdown (backwards). Explain to students how to record for replay:

a) Speak clearly and thoughtfully to your subconscious on the counting up, making sure that each number is recorded.

b) Listen to the sound of each number as you speak it.

c) Keep the beat going, don't miss a count.

d) Clap, or perform some muscular action (such as a leg-slap or snap) on each number as you speak it.

e) On the top number reached in each series, let go; turn the countdown job over to your subconscious, speaking and clapping and listening to your voice, enjoying yourself.

On the students' first try, their recorded countdown may stop suddenly. This indicates that the concentration going up was not sufficient, nor focused strongly enough to make the necessary imprint for playback. Try it again, aiming for deeper concentration.

Synonyms/Antonyms: A Pass-Around Game

Class selects one word such as, "large." In rhythm, class chants the word in half-notes. One student answers with a synonym of large. Class chants again, and the next student answers with another synonym. The idea is to see how long this can go on without repeating a synonym and without losing a beat. Team I members do the synonyms for the first word. Team II members do the next word. By giving 2 beats to each sound, there is time to think, but not too much time. Try the same procedure with antonyms.

Word Series

The learning time for any word series, such as "planets," can be shortened with a rhythmic setting and muscular reinforcement:

Clap — x x x x x x x x
Speak — Mercury, Venus, Earth, Mars, Jupiter, Saturn, Neptune, Pluto.
or "minerals":

Clap — x x x x x x x x
Speak — Iron, Aluminum, Manganese, Copper, Zinc, Lead, Silver and Gold.

After a number of examples have been done with the class, many students will begin to resolve their own learning tasks in this manner and in a shorter time than before.

Longitude versus latitude

The meaning of these words becomes clear by expressing each word—
a) with mouth formation:
"Longitude"—say and feel the mouth motion.
"Latitude"—what mouth shape is the word?
b) with arms.
c) with body:
From a low position (longitude) jump as high as possible.
Stretch (latitude) and widen.

OTHER LEARNING AIDS
contributed by Mrs. Minerva Cook, classroom teacher, Lowell School, Mesa, Arizona

Language arts

Rhythmic Spelling of new words by syllable. EXAMPLE: beau—ti—ful

a) Clap each letter in rhythm: b - e - a - u - t - i - f - u - l

b) On capital letters, clap overhead.

c) On a silent "e" at end of a word fold hands over silently.

d) After an introduction, move around the room to accompaniment of xylophone, clapping and spelling words as you move.

e) On a difficult letter, accent it with a stronger clap and add a strong physical motion. This will reinforce the learning track to the brain and aid memory retention.

f) Write the word with a toe—"in sand"

   Write the word in space with one or both arms

   Write the word on leg with one finger

On compass directions: "North, South, East and West."

a) Teacher: "Finger trace on your paper to the top." Class speaks, "This is North." T: "To the bottom," Class—"This is South." T: "To the right edge," "This is east" and t: "to the left edge," Class: "This is West."

b) "Close your eyes and do the same;

   Ready now to play the game?"

   "To the top"   Class: "This is North."   etc.

c) Select different crayons and make a design on paper moving your crayon according to the directions given and the rhythmic pattern played on a hand drum:

South | | ⊓ | ; West⊓ | | | ; East| ⊓ | | ; North⊓ | ⊓ |

d) Doing directions with body instead of on paper:

1) Reach your hands over head for north.	Class speaks, "North"
Touch the floor for south.	"South"
Reach out to right for east.	"East"
Reach out to left for west.	"West"

Leader speaks:

2) Reach North———South———East———West———etc.

e) Doing map directions on your stomach or standing up:

1) "Let your fingers touch your hair,
   Go on north, catch a polar bear!"

   "Right hand stretches and dips in the ocean (Atlantic)
   Left hand stretches to Pacific a-floatin'."

   "Pull up your feet, in the air, if you please;
   Now let them down and stretch out 'til you freeze!" (Antarctic)

2) "Pull in your arms and take up the slack,
   Roll yourself over on to your back.
   Go traveling again and you are the map,

Reach to the North, to the white bear's lair;
Take me clear South, penquins are there
Eastward, I wish, to Atlantic, a dip—
Leftward and westward—toward Pacific, a trip.''

f) *Clockwise and counter-clockwise*
Clockwise:
"Notice how the clock hands move—
This is clockwise; clap and speak it (''clockwise'')
Sit down on your knees, please, and find your 12 o'clock on the floor.
Trace it please, from your home-base store.
To the drum beat, to each hour
Start on one and pivot 'round
Clockwise moving; 12 beats sound.
Speaking numbers, tapping round.'' (Play a steady, not fast, 12 beats)

Counter Clockwise:
"Can you start at 12 again?
And counting backwards 'round your clock,
Tap each number: do not stop
Until you reach the hour, ''one''—
Speaking, tapping with the drum?

"You have now moved counter-clockwise.
(Just opposite from the hands you see inside the clock—)
Let's make a circle, like a clock
We are the hands, we'll step the hours
Clockwise go—from one to twelve————(SPEAK AND STEP)
Now counter-clockwise, twelve to one.''

"Step with the drum and call out the numbers
Here we go around together
Clockwise————
Turn around—and go counter-clockwise.''

Two Circles—Inside circle (girls), triangle-leader starts and stops motion. Outside circle (boys), drum-leader starts and stops motion. Each circle moves one direction only but must depend on their leaders for starting and stopping.

g) *Letter Form in Movement* (Contributed by Minerva Cook)

Game:

1) Have an enlarged letter-model showing in front of room.
2) Class becomes a human typewriter, forming the roller carriage, and the sheet of paper: 2 lines across room— ————
————

3) The two lines will now move as one body for margins, and indentations for Heading, Salutation, Body and Ending.

4) Decide on muscular signals for capitals, commas and periods such as: clap for capital letters, stamp for period and a hip-swish for commas, etc.

5) Class reads each line aloud in unison; moves accordingly to make indentations, line margins correctly, etc. Teacher uses triangle trill at end of each line to indicate end of line and roller-carriage return.

Rhythmic-Muscular Coordination not only aids learning but it also frees the student to learn more easily and faster.

DEVELOPING CONCENTRATION, FOCUS AND LISTENING ATTENTION

A rhythmic pattern tossed into the air draws attention. The focus is immediate and concentration begins.

A school auditorium was packed with children waiting for their assembly program to begin and their guest speaker was late. The students became noisier and noisier until the din grew to a raucous uproar. Teachers stood up uneasily and looked frowningly at the students. Even the Principal seemed not to know how to silence the crowd, when a

young teacher stepped to the front and clapped loudly: ♩ ♩ ♫♩ ♩ For an instant

the silence was jolting! Then an answer rang out across the auditorium, ♩ ♩ ♫♩ ♩ as a hundred children clapped in unison.

Miss Rapley clapped another phrase and this time all five hundred children answered her.

Together they developed rhythmic ensembles, then put rhythms with songs. The uproar and confusion had changed into focused listening, concentration and exciting results. When the guest arrived, no time was lost and the students were alert, relaxed and ready.

EXTENDING THE LISTENING AND CONCENTRATION SPAN

a) Through rhythmic content (interest).

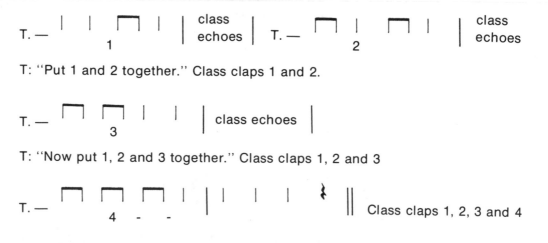

T: "Put 1 and 2 together." Class claps 1 and 2.

T: "Now put 1, 2 and 3 together." Class claps 1, 2 and 3

Notice longer phrase in #4.

NOTE: This much could not be retained without several practices. The idea is to make each session successful and a stretching one for every student. Because of the appeal of rhythm, he listens and his hearing, listening attention and focus improve.

   b) Adding a text helps to clarify and accelerate the learning and memory retention:

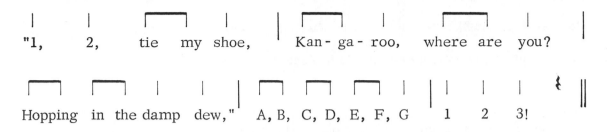

"1,   2,   tie   my   shoe,   Kan - ga - roo,   where   are   you?

Hopping   in   the damp   dew,"   A, B, C, D, E, F, G   1   2   3!

INCREASING DEPTH OF CONCENTRATION WITH

a) Rhythm Sequences with Speech.

Games

   1) Use the last phrase in II - B, continue the alphabet to the end, clapping and speaking.

Group I: A   B   C   D   E   F   G,   H   I   J

Group II: K   L   M   N   O   P   Q,   R   S   T

Group I: U   V   W   -   X   Y   Z

   2) Use an alternating sequence of alphabet and numbers based on a 4—beat pattern:

clap: | | | | | | | | | | | | | | | | | | | | | | | |
speak: A B C D   1 2 3 4   E F G H   5 6 7 8   I J K L   9 10 11 12

   3) Divide the class into 2 groups. Group I speaks the alphabet in four beats answered by Group II speaking the numbers backwards.
   4) Group I challenges Group II to do both parts without losing a beat.
   5) Try saying alphabet backwards, numbers forwards.
   6) Change the pattern to five beats each.
   7) Anyone for a six-beat sequence?

   b) Changing Meter Sequence with alphabet and percussion (stamp/clap). *Preparation*: Using a stamp as the stressed beat, start with alternating pattern: Stamp—Clap—Stamp—Clap—Clap, say the alphabet.

Games

1) The leader changes number of claps to follow the stamp as follows:

stamp—clap—stamp—clap. ‖ stamp—clap—clap, stamp—clap—clap. ‖

Leader calls the change for next sequence as:

stamp—clap, | stamp—clap—clap, | stamp—clap—clap—clap. ⫶‖ (repeat)

The idea is to have no pauses or lost beats. The caller must be able to speak out while he and the class are doing a sequence.

2) Using a one-clap / two-clap sequence, say the alphabet with it. Establish the sequence several times so that it can be carried on by the subconscious.

c) Singing with Muscular Rhythmic Patterns.

Games

1) Using two tones only, Yoo-hoo or So-Me, decide which of the tones So or Me will be sung with the stamp action: the other tone will go with the clap. Establish the pattern

    | | |

first— stamp, clap-clap, then add the alphabet singing.

2) Try a two-three beat sequence. Change the note sung on the stamp.

3) Divide in two groups to sing in canon. Second part begins after two beats.

4) Try a three-beat sequence. Establish a two-beat singsong So—Mi ostinato for the voice doing the alphabet.

d) Try a rhythmic pattern (ostinato) against a longer rhythmic line and add speech.

Games

1) Hearing exercise: A volunteer selects a wood block or other percussion instrument for a rhythmic pattern. This is played against the teacher's longer rhythmic line. The object of the game is to see how long he can keep this pattern going without changing it or losing a beat. Class listens, trying to hear both parts. At any change heard in the wood block pattern, class raises hands and players must stop. Purpose is to stimulate deeper and more focused listening. Next person's turn. Intersperse with class trying a soft two-finger clap with the pattern.

2) Inner hearing with alphabet. Using the rhythmic pattern: (clap)— | | ⌐⌐ |

(feet)— ♩ ♩ ♫ ♩ , speak and clap, A B C D E, (F G H I J). Repeat the same pattern with the feet and *think* the letters, do not speak them; the next five letters clap and speak followed by thinking the letters to the foot pattern. Do NOT lose a beat. Try it with other rhythmic patterns.

3) Partner game—Establish a rhythmic pattern with both partners doing the same pattern. After this pattern is established, partner A begins talking freely, not in rhythm, telling partner B what he likes best to do. The idea is to keep the rhythmic pattern going

without the speech affecting or changing it. B then replies either asking A questions about what A has said or adding his favorite pastime.

Any subject of interest can be used. Although this may be exceedingly difficult at first, it is an intriguing game even outside of school. Let a few weeks go by, then try it again. Achieving this brings about a release for each student and an awareness that he is more able than before and ready for ever greater challenges. Moreover, the rhythmic pattern, when recorded by the conscious mind, can be carried out by the subconscious while the speaking goes on independently and freely.

e) Carrying out one line in imitation of itself. (duet by one person) (A challenging mental / memory / muscular / listening-doing exercise.)

Game—(Class takes a familiar canon such as "Frère Jacques.")

1) Sing the first phrase (2 measures) and stop.
2) Clap the words you have just sung.
3) Sing the next phrase then clap it.
4) Next 2 measures and clap the words.
5) Finish song and clap words.
6) Begin the song again continuing to end. On the second phrase begin clapping the words you have already sung.

Game—(Try other songs such as, "Hot Cross Buns," "Swanee River," "Row, Row, Row Your Boat," etc. Clapping canon begins one measure after song starts.)

Outcomes of such muscular coordination and mind stretching games should become evident in increased academic achievements and easier, faster learning. Not only because these games are enjoyable but because *in music* and its ingredients lie more disciplines and demands on all of one's faculties than are possible in any one academic subject or all subjects.

Developing Listening Acuity and Memory Through Association of Sound Textures and Movement Directions.

(a) Obstacle Course Game:[2] (Two teams)
1) Set up four contrasting sounds such as wood block, metal chair-tapped, drum, and glockenspiel (one note).
2) Select one sound for each direction as:
wood block—one step forward
glock—one step backward
metal chair-tapped—one step to left
drum—one step to right
3) The entire class practices with two signals such as forwards and backwards; then three signals and finally four signals to make sure they understand the sound signals.
4) Set up an obstacle course across front of room, using chairs, stands, etc.
5) Team I—Captain and Director.
Captain is blindfolded and placed at starting point. His goal is to reach the goal post without touching any of the objects or obstacles enroute. He must move only as directed

[2] This game was introduced at the ORFF (AOSA) Symposium Demonstration in Memphis, Tenn. in 1971 by Sandra Skyhar of Toronto, Canada.

by the sounds he hears. Director from the same team directs the players accordingly, leading the captain around the obstacles step by step toward the goal post. If the Captain touches an obstacle, both are out, "no point", and Team II takes the turn.

Cumulative team scores can be kept over a month. This is a good rainy day game or relief change from academic work. At each new period, select four new sounds to extend the hearing discrimination and memory focus.

Everyone is creative by nature. Two or more minds working together can be more creative than one; therefore, it is logical also that one idea generates and sparks another. This sharing of ideas, techniques and principles is as vital to improvement and relevancy of education as it is to Science and Medicine.

Whatever a teacher comes upon that helps children to find out more about themselves and their environment should be shared with others.

CHAPTER 4

The Singing Voice

The child, by nature, would sing before speaking, except that our culture negates this. The mother's voice represents melody to her infant in the natural movement and sense of well-being that it evokes. In cases where the mother actually sings lullabies, holds and rocks her baby, the child will often sing and coo his responses long before using his speaking voice.

Singing is an extension of speech. The singing voice is capable of expressing more nuanced emotions than the speaking voice. It thus adds dimension to speech. The three-tone chant is universal to childhood; it is inherent at birth and, like rhythm, implies the need to be developed and expressed.

Although this growing muscle is not yet strong enough to produce the three tones at birth, by early years and kindergarten age the child is readily using it to express his thought in stream-of-consciousness fashion, by teasing and through calling games. Logically, the young child should be engaged in singing conversations and rhymes using his three tones to exercise and secure his voice.

Singing aids the speaking voice by prolonging vowel duration, connecting the consonant with the vowel that follows, and by lending a tonal inflection and phrase-flow so vital to oral reading. The resonant quality in singing should be carried over into a resonant speaking voice.

Because this first step is so widely neglected in the home, in the nursery and kindergarten, young voices have little opportunity to establish a foundation of pitch security. Although some children appear to sing TV songs of wide range by imitation, they very soon lose this imitative talent and fall into talking a song, like the child who is sitting beside them. When the child reaches six or seven, it becomes doubly difficult to re-establish a foundation of pitch placement and send the young voice on its way.

Hand signals[1] are a rich blessing and reinforcement for knowledgeable singing at

---

[1] The origin is thought to be in England with James Curwen who published them in 1860. These were specific hand designs for each tone of the diatonic scale. Zoltan Kodaly and colleagues in Hungary have combined these signals with the American movable "do" in the successful Hungarian Singing Schools and their state-wide music education system.

any age, but especially so at this time. Now he can figuratively "see" and direct his own instrument. These specific and spatial muscular designs offer children game-like skill development in pitch placement and control, provide an opportunity to create their own tunes and to direct or lead their songs. Tonal memory, understanding of intervals and inner hearing develop with these hand signals. (See diagram below.)

HAND SIGNALS FOR SYLLABLES

Singing with Hand Signals becomes a game that produces singing skills. This game is enjoyed by children of all ages because it provides a physical symbol for each tone and that tone's function in the scale or song. The Hand Signals are also a rhythmic aid to singing, to conducting and to musicality.

The instrumental ostinati can be introduced with Hand Signals and voices, then transferred to the instruments.

Introduce the songs with Hand Signals—syllables.

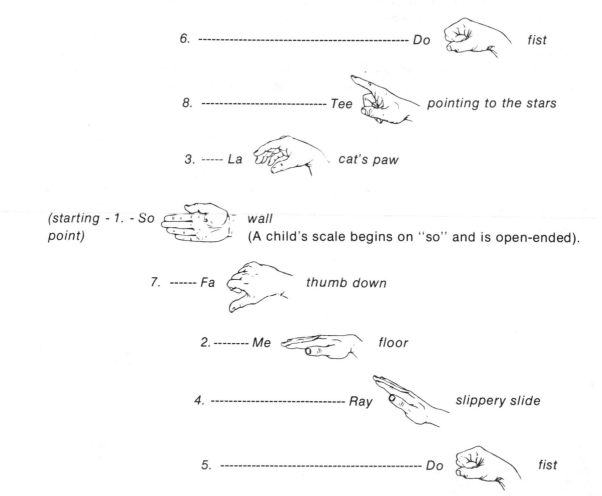

6. --- Do   *fist*

8. -------------------------- Tee   *pointing to the stars*

3. ----- La   *cat's paw*

(starting - 1. - So   *wall*
point)   (A child's scale begins on "so" and is open-ended).

7. ------ Fa   *thumb down*

2. -------- Me   *floor*

4. ---------------------------- Ray   *slippery slide*

5. ------------------------------------- Do   *fist*

Singing begins with awareness and is both teachable and learnable. The ability to sing is essential to a child's well-being, *now* and *later* in his life.

Educational Goal

Therefore an achievement goal for the child in the early years (kindergarten and 1st grade especially) is to find, feel and use his singing voice, within a five to six-tone range, omitting the half-steps—"fa" (h) and/or "tee."

If one takes into account the writings of Palestrina, modern research by the Pillsbury Foundation Studies, educational work of Hill, Kodaly, and Orff, and recent research on the child's voice in Czechoslovakia[2], it would seem wise to exercise and secure the young voice within his three to five-tone range, but from different starting pitches. This voice process:

1) extends his range gradually while strengthening the voice muscle and the understanding of pitch relationships within a given range. An abundance of exploration can now take place. Within these singable boundaries there can be *knowledgeable manipulation* of his voice.

2) permits simultaneous development of muscular coordination in patterned accompaniments with the singing. These patterned accompaniments are short repeated phrases called "ostinati."

3) extends aural awareness and discrimination as *different* sound textures and registers in percussion instruments are introduced with the singing.

The psychological organization required, amounts to a self-stretching performance-development of ability to hear an increasing number of levels of moving sound patterns. He is coordinating his own part with the whole and at the same time singing the longer song melody.

The opening of the child is like a flower, in a gestalt-like total growth. Why is this so? Perhaps because tonal sound affects acuity of all five senses, and the performance of the repeated pattern (rhythmic muscular action) activates the subconscious which he is using in play.

To analyze further, the act of repeating a rhythmic pattern, singing language and consciously listening to a number of accompanying patterns requires total involvement. Because the doing and the total sound (rhythmic and tonal) are irresistible forces which draw the child into participation, he is stretching his own potential to accomplish the feat.

The importance of simplicity in each and all of the ensemble parts as well as in the song text and range cannot be overstressed. In the simplicity itself lies the individual development!

PHONICS

How can singing aid the child's speech and reading skills?

Repeating an earlier statement that singing prolongs speech sounds, why not use singing aids to connect phonetic sounds in pronouncement of words? EXAMPLE: a one-syllable word such as, BEN.

[2] Findings of Czechoslovakian research are discussed in a doctoral thesis by Dr. Dorothy Wilson, Chico State College, Chico, California, on *The Child's Voice* in which the natural range of the young child's voice is five tones *only*.

Instead of sounding each letter separately, use a singing tone to carry the sound of the first letter—B, *into* E, into the N sound, thus feeling, expressing, and perceiving the relationship of each letter to the total word. In *speaking,* the single letter sound will not sustain into the next letter; by singing or intoning it, the letter sounds can be sustained and connected into the total word.

For many children, this activity provides the answer to their reading problem of not being able to connect letter by letter sounds into a total word sound.

It should be pointed out that this process of intoning also develops better breathing and lung expansion!

READING REVERSALS

Where language reading requires left to right eye movements, the child who has a different polarization might read more easily from right to left. While this is contrary to the logic of language reading, it can be done in music, both in rhythmic and melodic reading with syllables. Reading music backwards is not only fun to do, but also develops keener sight reading proficiency and facility, left to right.

It may help the student with a reversal problem to know what a reversal is. By deliberate experience with the reversing process he becomes more able to cope with his particular reversal and in some cases to overcome it.

PHRASE-FLOW

The rise and fall in question and answer phrases can be experienced in "so—me" (yoo-hoo) chant very early.

"Where are you?"   (S M S)
"I am here."   (S S M)

The awareness of the higher pitched ending of the question becomes a direct experience both in vocal sounds and spatial relationship of the two tones used with the hand signals. Combining this song reading with question and answer games, reinforces language inflection.

After making up their own tunes for a nursery rhyme using S—M and S—M—L, their awareness of phrase-flow and voice inflection automatically increases and may easily lead to exploration in changing accents, distorting the natural way of speaking a rhyme, even into a nonsense result. This is excellent.

To further stimulate awareness of voice inflection a familiar rhyme is set into melody and the melody is derived from the actual word inflection in each phrase of the rhyme. This can be done in class with different students saying the first line or phrase to locate the highs and lows expressed. As the class listens, they make their choice, and with a designated starting tone, such as "so," various students try singing or designating the phrase melody with hand signals. Building from this first phrase, the second phrase is added in similar fashion.

Here is an example of such a process and the setting that resulted at approximately fourth grade level:

> "Good better best ⌿,
> Never let it rest ⌿,
> 'Til your good is better ⌿,
> And your better best ⌿."

| | ⌐⌐ | ⌿ | ⌐ ⌐ | ⌿
S   M R M   S S M R M

⌐ ⌐ | | | ⌐ ⌐ | ⌿
S S L L D' L   S S M R M

Notice how the word "better" was changed to "bet—ter" in the melody to prolong the climax of the song. Moreover, it is interesting to note that they felt no pull to go down to "dō" at the end, nor at any other place. This is because the child's nature is not related to a "dō" tonality. He does not need a final "dō" to conclude his song. In his nature, the song is not ended, and in this way, he can return to it, repeat it, and/or extend it whenever and however he wishes.

Part of the importance of the pentatonic scale lies in its wonderfully natural application and adaptation to the child's nature. It is a floating free scale for exploration and innovation (without the pull of a leading tone that might force the piece to end). It is a scale with endless possibilities in combining parts, improvising, going new places without any fear of dissonant friction and without fear of failure to do the expected!

Singing an ostinato, such as S—M, against a longer melodic line, is an important experience that should be carried on again and again, gradually widening the tonal range and rhythmic content. This can be performed first in duets between individuals and small groups, making sure that both parts are heard by the singers; then in trios; two ostinati parts; one melody, etc.

These singing games, with the melodic line often improvised by the leader who hand signals, produce marked progress in vocal security and independence, hearing acuity and concentration. Again, the pentatonic scale is vital to the individual success and understanding.

EXAMPLE:

Ostinato: ♩   ♩ :|| and/or   ♩ ♩ ♩ ♩ :||
          S - M   M R M S

Hand
Signal |₄ ||| | | | | | | | | ♩ ♩ | ♩. ⌿ |
Melody   S S L S M R D M S - L - S - - -

TWO ECHO CHAIN GAMES WITH HAND SIGNALS

DIRECTIONS: Eight pairs of singers facing in two rows of four couples each. Couple No. 1 introduces the first phrase and waits for couple No. 2 to echo it before continuing to the next phrase. Each couple in turn echoes that phrase while a new phrase is being introduced. Upon reaching the final phrase each couple repeats it softly until all are singing in unison. Notice that each pair watches only the pair whom they echo. All keep a steady, even beat. This game produces 4-part singing.

I.

S	L	S	M	(echo)
S	M	S	S	_____
S	D'	S	D'	_____
D'	L	S	M	_____
S	M	M	S	_____
M	L	S	M	_____
M	D	M	S	_____
M	—	S	—	_____

II.

S	S	M	S	(echo)
S	S	D'	S	_____
S	D'	L	S	_____
M	S	M	D	_____
D	M	M	D	_____
S	D'	D'	S	_____
S	M	L	S	_____
M	—	S	—	_____

Mind stretching through inner hearing/silent singing

Start on "so."

1) Echo singing of phrases using hand signals. One team closes their eyes and listens while the other team sings a given or improvised phrase by leader. Team opens its eyes and repeats same phrase with hand signals.

2) Leader silently directs a phrase with hand signals and indicates starting pitch of "so." Class watches, then repeats, singing the same phrase with hand signals. This later evolves into a mystery song game with different volunteers doing the tune silently with hand signals as the class watches and tries to guess the song.

3) Singing a phrase backward. THIS IS DIFFICULT. Team I sings a given or directed phrase as Team II listens, eyes closed, then reproduces that phrase backwards.
EXAMPLE: I—S S M S L S   II—S L S M S S

4) Self-ostinato with a familiar song. With hand signals, form an ostinato, singing it for a few measures of introduction before adding the song. Continue the ostinato with hand signals and sing the familiar song.

5) Sing a familiar song and *clap* the same song starting two measures later than the

voice. This game requires on-going memory retention—having to memory-clap what one has already sung while continuing or carrying forward the song.

(a) Try vocal warm-ups using a pentatonic repeating sequence of L—S—M—R—D—R—M—S. Begin slowly, clapping softly for each tone; increase tempo and lightness with faster clapping into a relaxed but clear and fast singing in unison.

(b) Improvise a phrase with hand signals such as: S M S—L M M. On repeating the phrase, inflect the third tone "S" with a raised thumb—S M S SEE L M M. Have the class repeat it, using hand signals showing the So to See. Pitch So = G to G♯.

Practice using S—S♯—L in student leading of improvised phrases. Later, the third tone ME can be lowered a half step to MAY by crooking the index finger—a floor with index finger curved down. This shows physically and tonally that a sharp (♯) raises a tone a half-step and a flat (♭) lowers a tone a half-step.

Hexatonic scale

We have proceeded logically so far from S—M, S—M—L, L—S—M—R, L—S—M—R—D. Prior to the full diatonic scale of D R M F S L T D, should come a six-tone (hexachord) range, sometimes called hexatonic, L—S—F—M—R—D and chromatic alterations of "so" to "see," "me" to "may."

S L S (F) M R D. For the Fa(h) signal, make a fist with the thumb pointing to the floor. To feel the closeness of Fa(h) to Me, place the other hand in Me (floor) signal directly beneath the pointed down thumb of the Fa(h) signal, so that the thumb touches the back of the Me hand. Practice singing and forming the Fa and Me sequence—(see *Today with Music,* page 58.)

"See   how   they   run"__   (from *Three Blind Mice*)

S L S F M   D (from *Frère Jacques*)

Try to recall songs that contain S—F—M. . . .
"Jingle Bells,"   "Row, Row, Row your boat"

Now try making up a song using S—F—M in several places on this rhythmic line: Begin the song on So—

S

Ask a partner to sing it with you. Add a second melody part on half notes—

S

Try the two parts together. Make any changes to improve the sound and sing it again. Try sight-singing this melody, which adds color, passing tones to So and Me—

```
3
) S S#  | L   M   Mb | M     R M | F   M   R | S -
{                                                 }
  ⁐    |    D - --   |  D - - -  |  R - - -  | M -

  S S# | L  D'  L | S   M   R M | F   M   R | D -
{                                                 }
  ⁐    | F -- - - |  M - - - --- |  R - - --- | D -
```

Sing each part separately to assure accuracy. Sing in two parts, listening to both parts. Exchange parts.

Students and teacher should practice setting a number of rhythmic lines to hexatonic melodies, then explore possibilities for introducing color changes on Me and So.
WARNING: The danger of this will be in introducing it before the voice is secure and accurate with the student knowledgeable in his reading performance. It should be realized that most students will be capable of imitating the sound fairly well and can easily be *trained* by rote to sing these half steps. *Educating* him is quite a different process and produces knowledgeability as to the where, how and why of its use.

VOICE

Unless there is a handicap (physical defect in throat muscles, vocal chords) practically every child can learn to produce and control singing pitch.

PITCH INDEPENDENCE

Pitch independence means ability to maintain accuracy of melodic line against another part or parts, instrumental or vocal.

LISTENING AWARENESS

Listening awareness of tone changes and of pitch in individual singing is essential. Group singing for the children who have difficulties is no answer or solution. The longer they continue to "talk a song" the duller their perception of pitch becomes. For these children, begin with tone calls, echo singing matching another child; then individual singing with xylophone accompaniment to strengthen awareness of his own voice.

AIDS TO PITCH PLACEMENT AND CONTROL

1) Cupping an ear with one hand, and cupping the mouth with the other hand (telephone game). Sing an echo to another student's singing.

2) Whispering in a very high pitch the entire song text. The test of high whispering is raised eyebrows and a noticeable feeling of raising the roof of the mouth.

3) Teacher helps the student to sing higher by patting him under the chin or touching the top of his head to bring the tone upwards.

4) Student fills his chest with air and directs a "So - Me" or a single high tone toward an object on the ceiling.

5) Throw the head down between the knees as he sings a "G", "C", "A", etc. This sudden thrusting of the head down throws the sound into voice box of cheek bones and is often effective in raising the voice.

6) Avoid songs with extensive pitch range. Begin with So - Me - La in the middle range, singing different combinations of these tonal relationships. Use hand signal games led by the students to develop these skills.

7) Use of Hand Signals

CHAPTER 5

Speech

"Language must be considered inseparable from music and movement."
—Carl Orff

Speech, a basic means of communication, becomes a regulator of behavior. Where absence of speech may bring about violence, the presence of speech brings interaction and makes possible comparisons, evaluations and peaceful arbitrations.

L.S. Vigotsky, Russian psychologist, in his extensive researches[1] concluded that human mental development has its source in verbal communication between child and adult and later becomes the means of organization of the child's own behavior.

It begins with a word which defines an object and relates that object to a definite category.

Acquisition of verbal speech allows man to go beyond the visual perception of objects and scenes, into analysis of their data or components—bringing about a deeper reflection of his world.

Many of the elements, techniques and forms of musical composition can be first experienced by children in speech ensembles. Externalizing speech (oral), then internalizing the same line (thinking and carrying it silently), extend the disciplines of concentration and memory and sharpen the focus of attention.

The origin of musical form is speech.

BEHAVIORAL GOALS FOR S'EECH

The child demonstrates the ability to articulate and phrase his language ('   e inflection) with increasing enjoyment of the sounds and their various meanings:

—to explore possibilities in word selection and pronunciation.

—to articulate mouth sounds or separate syllables and to move (walk) while he is speaking.

—to speak his rhythmic verse-rhymes accompanying them with clap-snap etc. in a beat-pattern ostinato.

—to participate in question-answer phrases and to distinguish the differences in voice levels used.

—to develop and/or contribute to the forming of word chains in different categories.

—to speak a number of heritage (nursery and nonsense) rhymes, proverbs, sayings and to extend them into speech/action ensembles.

[1] *Speech and the Development of Mental Processes in the Child*, A.R. Luria and F. La. Yudovich.

57

—to organize rhythmic spelling of words, and other learning facts into rhythmic expression to facilitate his learning.

—to explore, recognize and use different voice levels.

—to utilize and express in speech ensembles many of the devices used in musical composition, and many of the common musical forms. (canon, rondo, etc.)

—to interpret poetry in sound and movement.

—to create or extend poetry.

—to enjoy his own language expression, creating new sounds, with heritage stories.

—to participate in setting and expressing given verse or phrase in melody (song) according to rise and fall of the syllables.

—to internalize known passages (rhymes) continuing the word line silently and speaking only the 1st and last words of the given rhyme. (inner hearing)

—to increase his listening and concentration span through rhythmic speech work.

—to improve his rhythmic muscular coordination through the combining of speech and muscular action.

—to bring about improvement in his well-being (freedom with control) through these daily experiences with rhythmic, muscular and speech expressions.

Exploring the voice for spontaneity in expression

From the first one-syllable sounds of infancy, the exploration of sound-making possibilities continues into the child's school years, at which point his spontaneity with language in street games and nonsense syllables is rather abruptly cut off as being silly! A growing reluctance to use them, except in play, results. His natural ear for language and his delight in its nuances and flow have been discouraged and dulled.

Let us re-sensitize his listening and re-kindle his zest for exploration of sounds with rhythmic expression in speech with added action.

1) *Nonsense syllables for nursery rhymes.*

Introduce and speak a familiar rhyme such as "Little Miss Muffet."

a) Using the same syllable rhythm, substitute "gobbledy gook" (nonsense talk) syllables and do the rhyme. Everybody tries at the same time to see what they can do (without the self-consciousness of a solo performance).

b) Choose another rhyme, say it together then substitute nonsense sounds. If different children wish to do one alone, splendid. Gradually, they will enjoy doing this.

c) For a change of pace—set aside three minutes for nonsense conversation.

2) *Exploring the voice levels*

a) Awareness of voice levels

What am I now doing with my voice?—speaking.

What am I doing now?—whispering.

And what is the opposite of a whisper?—shout or yell.

GAME: (Using the alphabet and a two-finger clap on the beat, to stay together)

1) Write the three words "speak—whisper—shout" on the board. (If the children are unable to read such words, use the open hand—three fingers—to represent the three levels.

——speak
——whisper
——shout

Pointing to one of the three words, everyone starts the alphabet, being careful to stay together. As they continue, change the level intermittently to indicate voice change. Repeat the game several times to develop more alertness and awareness.

2) Highest to lowest speaking tones—low, middle, high.

For very young children use the Big Bear, Middlesized Bear and Wee Bear's voice. Instead of the alphabet, counting up to ten or fifteen can be used. They stay together with a two-finger beat. Repeat the game placing one hand on the throat to feel the sensations, while the other keeps the beat with a leg pat.

3) The same game can be used with "whisper," perhaps only low and high. With this game comes a new awareness of the feeling of a very high whisper in the jowls, eyes and lifting of the eyebrows. This exercise of high whispering tends to raise the speaking levels of their voices and lightens the singing voice, even lifting it a few tones higher.

4) Going from the lowest possible voice sound to the highest possible sound in a familiar rhyme or saying, such as, "Early to bed, early to rise, makes a man healthy, wealthy and wise." Begin in a crouching position and extend upwards reaching gradually to the highest sound by the last word, "wise."

Other voice sounds—Plop   Yah   Whawsh   Splash   Poop   Dah
Hoo   Ffft   Skah   Hee   Kloo

1) Make a game out of such nonsense syllables, dividing the class into teams—one sound each. A leader directs; pointing to the different teams for their different sounds, in different sequences and together. Other volunteers direct the ensemble.

2) Class selects three contrasting syllables for everyone to use in any way they choose. The leader indicates the loud to soft degrees that he wants, also he can point to soloists for their performance, and indicate the end of the piece.

3) Class selects three contrasting syllables representing high, middle, low, for the volunteer director to indicate, using three fingers for the three levels, as to which level he wishes at any given time. As he opens and raises his hands, the loudness would increase, etc.

DEVELOPING A TASTE FOR LANGUAGE

Getting the "feel" of language begins with single words. Explore words that seem to have "taste" to their sounds like: marshmallows, crunchy, juicy, sour, brittle, jelly. Pay special attention to:

—words that seem to have a "feel" or "shape" in the mouth like: longitude, latitude, yawn, giggle, pop, scram, boom, dumpy.

—words that seem to have "character" in their sounds like: hawk, vulture, meadowlark, hummingbird, eagle, dove, crook, spook, monster, ogre, round, witch.

—that seem to have "texture" or color in their sounds like: raven, surf, soft snow, crystal, gutter, oil, sticky.

—that seem to have "action" in their sounds like: drag, smash, missile, arrow, molasses, kangaroo, plummeting, diving.

Like people, there are thin words, fat words, dumpy and grumpy words, long words, short words, slow and fast words, hard words, soft words, lovely and ugly words.

Playing with words and categories of words, opposites and alike, stimulates the imagination and brings about new dimensions of awareness and sensitivity. Draw from the class such descriptive words. An extension might be to use one such list of words in an original story as a spring board to creative writing.

Speech ensembles*

Rhythmic speech and musicality begin with nursery rhymes. A wealth of nursery rhymes expressed and enjoyed in infancy almost assures that child of being musical, moving with a linear flow and speaking with pleasing voice inflections. Nursery rhymes may even contribute to readiness in reading fluency.

Although children at intermediate age levels are not apt to be interested in Mother Goose Nursery Rhymes, they do need experience with rhythmic speech. Many children have had little or no association with heritage rhymes.

The answer is proverbs,[2] sayings, their counting out rhymes, and other verses which offer a wealth of material for experience in ensemble building, speech improvement, and understanding of compositional techniques leading into art form in poetry and music.

From one proverb used as a model for development, can come all kinds of creative ideas from the class, using their *own* texts and ensemble parts.

Building word chains in different categories; changing accents

Begin with word series in different categories, drawn from the class, and based on kinds of sounds (hard, soft; warm, cold; ugly, beautiful) either freely phrased or set into a rhythmic structure.
EXAMPLE: Birds. Contrasting sounds contained in their names.

1) Hard sounds: "Crow, Hawk, Eagle, Vulture!" Repeat this series several times exaggerating the hardness or harshness in the names.

2) Soft or mellow sounding names that describe other birds such as: "Meadowlark, Bobolink, Hummingbird, Dove." Repeat this series for mellow sounds.
—Team I speaks first series with staccato harshness.
—Team II replies with deliberate mellowness in word sounds.
—Team I expresses the series without speaking; only in clapping sounds that become louder with each name.
—Team II replies with name clapping that becomes softer and slower toward last name.
 A third time through could be done in movement and/or words.

Develop rhythmic ensembles based on categories as baseball teams; states and capitols; names of streets, schools, teachers, students, local police force, town officers, school board; rivers; products; favorable menus; soft drinks; weather. With each series develop a climax—go somewhere!

Local and pertinent material brings content and student together! Add a percussion ostinato (rhythmic pattern) taken from one word in series.

*See Rhythmic Speech Ensembles, G.C. Nash
[2] Proverbs are said to contain the wit and values of a nation, in fewer words than expected.

(snap)	(clap)	(leg pat)	(stamp)
x x	x x	x x	x x
Cold weather,	hot weather,	windy weather,	stormy weather,

F   O   G!

pp ∿∿∿∿∿

(dark, intoned chant)   (rub hands and spread slowly outwards)

Notice how the voices must rise, even accelerate, then suddenly, darken into a soft and spreading sound on F   O   G!

Percussion sounds can be added (with or following each weather) if desired.

EXAMPLE: Cold weather (claves)   Hot weather (triangle)

Windy weather (fingernails on hand drum)

Stormy weather (timpani)   F   O   G (alto met. or soft cymbal)

Sayings or rhymes with changing accents:

EXAMPLE: "A penny saved is a penny earned."

1) Find the four beats: penny, saved, penny, earned. Accent strongly the first beat. Move over the accent one beat with each repetition of the saying. Listen to the sound. Reinforce the accented word with a hand clap.

2) Two Teams: Team I begins; Team II joins on the second time but accents the first beat while Team I moves the accent over to the second beat. Reinforce accents with hand clap. Add a walking of the beats.

Word chains in changing meter: (Sports category)

Using a foot tap or stamp for the down beat, change the meter according to the number of syllables in the words.

2-syllables: $\frac{2}{}$ Base - ball, |foot - ball, |base-ball, | foot- ball. |

$\frac{3}{}$ Bad-min - ton, |Bas-ket-ball, |Vol-ley-ball, | Soccer! |

(Could this chain be spoken completely in 2-meter?)

Transfer this word series into movement in place—

(swing right)   (clap) (swing left)   (clap)

Speak   Base - ball,   foot - ball,

Base - ball,   foot - ball,

(swing right - clap - clap) (swing left - clap - clap)

"Bad - min - ton,   bas - ket - ball,

Vol - ley - ball,   S O C C E R! (clap right and left)

SUBJECT: On Driving[3]

EXAMPLES: "A reckless driver seldom goes to jail." ▬

(4 beats of action/sound) Repeat the saying.

"Better late down here than early up there." ▬‖

(4 beats of silent action, then repeat the saying.)

Shorter sayings that were added to the above by a fifth level class—

"Watch the other guy!" —▬—

—▬—"Fasten your seatbelts!"

These four parts joined the ensemble, each group indicating sound or action for their respective parts. After building it, the climax was a screeching of brakes and cymbal crashes, followed by sudden silence in which the silent arm actions of "climbing up" or "climbing down" took place. (Some treading downwards!)

After doing a speech ensemble (rhythmic word series or a proverb with accompanying ostinati), transfer the rhythmic content of the words to hand drums or other percussion instruments, (clap, snap, etc. can be used) and perform the ensemble as a percussion composition. This involves inner hearing and intense concentration from students and develops:

1. keener awareness of rhythmic line.
2. word sounds, accents, and flow (phrasing).

EXAMPLES of proverbs to transfer to hand drums:

"Come what   may,   to-mor-row is   an- oth-er day."

a) "Come what may, to-mor-row is an-oth-er day."

Say it several times to find the rhythmic essence, then try to express it on the hand drum without speech.

b) "A stitch in time, saves nine."

c) "You may delay but time will not."

NOTE: Each student may express the proverb at hand in a different style, different inflection, accents, and phrasing. To explore these possibilities in one proverb is more valuable to awareness of speech, diction and phrase-flow, than doing many proverbs without exploration.

The proverb, "You can't have your cake and eat it, too," was developed into the following ensemble by one class.[4]

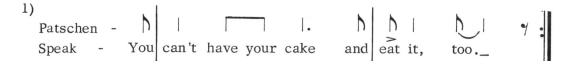

1)
Patschen -
Speak - You can't have your cake   and eat it,   too.

[3] In ten minutes, this is what one class did with the two sayings. Each group would naturally develop a given proverb differently. That's the exciting part for the teacher.

[4] St. Peter's Parochial School—St. Paul, Minnesota. Sister Conleth Hager—Music Instructor

2)

Clap -

Speak - Take the | good with the bad, take the | bad with the good.

3)

Sticks -

Speak - Fros - ting, fros - ting, | cho-co-late, yum, yum, yum.

4)

Stamp -

Speak - Pain - pain - | pain - pain.

a) Each group says its part twice, in turn 1, 2, 3, 4.

b) Group (1) says the proverb and continues repeating it.

c) Group (2) enters.

d) Group (3) enters.

e) Group (4) does not enter *until* Group (3) has said their part twice.

f) Each part continues speaking until the ending (coda) is stated in unison! Dynamics are developed and determined by the class.

Here is an example of a saying on physical fitness as done by another class in the same school:

"After supper take a walk."

Start with four circles, each with their selected instruments in the middle of the circles. Each circle does the action to fit their text.

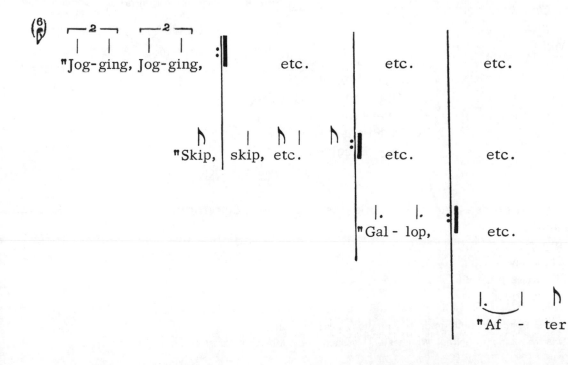

"Jog-ging, Jog-ging,   etc.   etc.   etc.

"Skip, | skip, etc.   etc.   etc.

"Gal - lop,   etc.

"Af - ter

sup-per,___ walk___ a mile"___ - Repeat . . . .

After saying (4) has been repeated 4 times, all circles stop and shout together, "DIET!"

POETRY

Creative writing of poetry and interpreting poetry with sound, movement and colors, should begin in the early years and continue into the middle and upper grades through high school.

There are many springboards and form structures to guide students in their creative development.

A. Japanese Haiku: 3-line format consisting of 5 syllables—7-syllables—5-syllables.

SNOW*
The trees capped with white
Its presence has hushed the world
A lone fox goes by.   (W. Levy)

A BOOK*
A book is a door
When its' opened, it's knowledge
When closed, memories.   (M. McWamana)

B. Cinquains: 5 lines, often in a diamond design—
1. Word subject or category—
2. Describing words—
3. Words describing action—
4. Words of feeling—
5. One word coming out of that category—

"Cats*
Frisky, fluffy
Playing with string,
Feeling cozy, warm,
Calico"

Linda Morotta

EXAMPLE 2:

"Ocean**
Surfing, splashing
Waves roaring, crashing
Feeling happy, all alive
Laughter."

Marshall Hinton

C. Short phrases can be springboards to creative poetry writing:
"In summer you can . . . . ."
"Spring is . . . . ."
"If I could fly . . . . ."
"Rain makes me feel . . . . ."
"I want to . . . . ."

* from Mrs. Reinhardt's 6th graders—Arlington, Massachusetts.

** Poems from Lincoln School, Winchester, Massachusetts. M. Harkins, Instructor, Grade Two.

D. WORD PICTURES

Ask each student to make a list of word pictures for each of the following topics. (One phrase for each topic)

"Walking alone on a beach at sunset."

"Full moon in the canyon."

"A haunted house at midnight."

"On the circus lot before the opening show."

"My first trip on a surf board."

Noticeable will be the unity of thought expression represented on each paper when read as one unit of poetry, rather than a series of responses to different topics. A number of beautiful poems should result.

E. With each of these poems, there could be sound interpretations by other students; movement (single or group) interpretation, and/or a painting interpretation of the poem.

F. Taking one poem as their inspiration model such as "Dream Dust" by Langston Hughes, one class developed their own poem entitled, "Moon Dust" to introduce their improvised opera, "Legend of the Moon Walk."

G. Try rhythmic accompaniments with rhythmic poetry.

H. A book that abounds in ideas that generate creativity in writing is Edna Gilbert's "A Way With Words." (See Bibliography)

Mouth muscle exercise

Do each exercise three to five times.

1) Make the inside of mouth as large an opening as you can (open the door), then close.
2) Open the mouth wide and smile. Relax.
3) Say—"lo——ngltude"; "la——litude". Say "Oh!", say "Wow!"
4) Use upper lip to cover lower lip. Relax.
5) Stretch lower lip up and over upper lip. Relax.
6) Fold both lips inward and smack them. Relax.
7) Squeeze lips into a kissing focus and make a smacking sound. Relax.
8) Stick out tongue as far as possible. Relax.
9) Explore with tongue over upper teeth and gums as if trying to find a piece of food. Relax.
*10) Touch nose to feel vibrations and say, "May, may, me, me, my, my, no, no, new, new, thing." Take away the touch and repeat the above.
*11) Keeping these sounds in the same frontal location as in # 10, say, "Lay, lay, lee, lee, lie, lie, low, low, lie, lie, low, low, lie, lie, low, low."

Speech exercises

From diaphragm: Say four times—*"F F T."* (as word "foot")

THEN—Whisper these words: Full - Fail - Feel - Follow

THEN—Deep laughter from the diaphragm.

Say three times: "Rough and tough puffed enough."

TH as in "thin"—breathe out over the tongue.

TH as in "that"—send the voice or sound out over the tongue.

*All of these exercises should also be intoned, (a comfortable singing tone) so that they flow from one to the other.

Say—"With tip of the tongue, touch the edge of your teeth,
Upper front teeth, with the tip of your tongue."
Say three times: "These teeth"
    WH—Round the lips and do a glide over the sound.
Say slowly: "Who - What - When - Which"
         Say: "White whales whipped and whistled through their whiskers."
    P—"Paper puppy puppets,
Pale pumpkins ask for pizzas,
  Pay a penny for the pepper piper,
    Pop it into pieces."
    B—"Bobby bit a blackbird,
Bobbling on the bench;
  Bobby blowing bubbles,
    Sitting on the fence."

Changing accents

Move over the accent one beat with each repetition of this old rhyme. The beats are marked (/)

"A sailor to his captain said,

'To sail on Friday, I've a dread.

I wish on Thursday you would go' -,

But the captain sailed on Friday".

CHAPTER 6

Notation

INTRODUCTION

Although the subject of notation is treated in a number of chapters, a separate one on the hows, whys and whens of notation is needed to help bring the specifics of notation into the classroom and to help teachers realize that reading music is both learnable and teachable. This skill should be among the child's basic rights in education toward a richer and freer adult life.

As teachers I believe we have caused some of the frustrations of students who are handed a trumpet or a violin (art form instrument) without any previous musical experience. It is too much to do all at once—trying to comprehend abstract symbols and producing specific tones on a difficult instrument in a rhythmic line. Is it any wonder that the casualties are so high and the disappointments often so deep as to cause the student to turn off music forever?

Music making at an early stage with easy-to-play tonebar and percussion instruments, should *precede* the use of art form instruments. The system of notation is expressed, presented and understood *before* art form instruments are introduced. I feel this should be introduced on a daily basis, rather than in a subsidiary once-a-week exposure.

If music literacy is achieved by every student in the public schools in Hungary, then certainly we can bring it about in America! And with creative freedom and responsibility on the part of the individual.

BEFORE NOTATION

A linear, flowing introduction to notation begins with speech rhymes and sayings, body percussion (clap, snap, etc.) and movement, and with classroom instruments. This precedes the use of written symbols. (See *Today with Music, Teacher's Annotated Edition*, by Grace Nash, pages III-XIII Alfred Publishing Co.)

1) Finding and expressing the phrased beat in the speech games, then transferring these language phrases (every syllable) into the hands with clapping, leg patting, and mallets on the tonebar instruments, prepare the way for notation symbols.

2) Using speech terms and phrases, as well as walking, running, pausing and stretching to express note values in order to articulate and "feel" their meaning, brings understanding into the written symbols.

NOTATION GOALS

What should be the goals in accomplishment with regard to reading music? What can the student achieve in this approach? Here is a check list of questions for instructors' self-evaluations:

"Can my students demonstrate the ability to":

1) Read by phrase rather than in a halting note-to-note fashion?

   a) See and interpret pitch relationships on the staff rather than single and separate pitches?

   b) See and interpret the rhythmic line or phrase rather than single, unrelated note values?

2) Use speech keys or terms for note values and thereby articulate a rhythmic line against a phrased beat, without hesitation, in combinations of eighth, quarter, half and whole notes, and corresponding rests that are not complex?

3) Use *so-fa* syllables (with movable *do* system) and specific hand signals for these syllables, and thereby sing at sight a pentatonic melody on a five-line staff with acceptable accuracy in rhythm using quarter, half and whole notes and corresponding rests in combinations that are not complex?

4) Take oral or written dictation of clapped phrases (one, two or three measures in length) using eighth, quarter, half and whole notes in easy combinations?

5) Notate the rhythmic content of a simple rhyme or saying? (e.g.: "Come out and play.")

6) Transcribe to the staff a melody given in *so-fa* syllables, provided that the starting tone is on a given line or space?

7) Play given notation (not complex) on the tonebar instruments, either from *so-fa* syllables or from staff notation and transfer a *so-fa* melody to letter names on the instruments?

PROCEDURES AND SEQUENCE FOR NOTATION

There are many ways to introduce notation. One sequential program for the young student is followed in the book *Today With Music* in which noteheads for beats are placed

on a two-line staff RIGHT  for performance with leg pat, clap-
LEFT

ping, clap and leg pat, claves, claves and hand drum, and finally to *so-me* with singing. (See pages 4-9.)

The silent quarter beat or rest is introduced with the word "rest". Then stems are added to the notes and space relationships are shown with a three-line staff:

Meanwhile, new percussion instruments are added one at a time and combined in ensembles. Eighth notes are shown and expressed in their relationship to quarter notes, in sayings and speech terms, *(Tee-Tee).* (See page 16, *Today With Music).* Each new symbol (and sound) is immediately incorporated in an ensemble game, along with movement games and techniques.

The next step is using rhythmic notation with note stems only in problem solving games:

      | | ⊓ |

(See page 17, *Today With Music)*

Half notes are shown and used in relation to quarters and eighths in speech, song and with instruments on two-line and three-line staffs. Three pitch tones, *so-me-la,* are practiced with hand signals in song and with an added xylophone accompaniment plus rhythm instruments. The *ostinato* (repeating pattern), is explained and combined with singing in a muscular pattern and tonal patterns. This engages and stretches the student's faculties and concentration much more than can be done in an academic subject.

Letter names for pitch are brought into relationship to the syllables *(so-fa)* through the tonebar instruments. The visual, hearing and muscular faculties are brought together, working simultaneously, reinforcing the track to the brain in a multi-media, multi-dimensional experience.

Rather than trying to read pitch in an *up and down* motion on a five-line staff, the rhythmic experience in speech, movement and tonebar instruments brings a *linear* flow to the reading, a musical performance rather than a rigid and vertical one. The importance of repetition in two and three-tone singing from the staff, plus a not-too-rapid progression into wide ranges of pitch, make for real satisfaction and steady accomplishment for the student.

Improvisation on the instruments, with speech, movement and body percussion, should be a daily experience, as he uses the ingredients and knowledge he already has in order to produce new arrangements, extensions and contrasts to the learned material. Here again is the need for specifics and boundaries (to prevent floundering or giving up) to encourage exploration, imagination and development of skills. Pentatonic (floating scales) allow and encourage such exploration and success in ensemble and solo work. They also provide the foundation for an understanding of diatonic and whole tone scales, jazz and the modes.

THE RECORDER

Introducing the soprano recorder crystallizes and accelerates sight reading skills, and with its tone duration and finger articulation requirements, prepares the way for art form instruments. It is also a lifetime instrument to be played in ensemble with its family of alto, tenor and bass recorders. It is beautiful with the tonebar and percussion instruments and should be a part of classroom music throughout school years. A good recorder can bring fine progress in reading and music literacy.

"Singing whatever we play," is a good policy to follow with the recorder. Improvisation practice, first in G and C pentatonic scales, then in modes and jazz scales, belongs in the recorder program as well as chamber music experience. (See *Recorder for Beginners; Recorder Ensembles,* by G.C.N.)

NOTATION AIDS AND GAMES

The stumbling blocks so often encountered in presenting notation are really unnecessary if experience with the ingredients precedes the written symbols; also, if the material or symbols are stated and shown in clear media which can be put to use in problem solving games and ensembles. For example:

A) Noteheads on the staff* Everyone has a note. Your head is your note.

You can make it a line note, or a space note, Using your two hands,

can you make a space note? A line note?

B) Staff lines When drawing a five-line staff or a two-line staff on the board, start

it from the bottom line and go upwards $\begin{matrix} 3 \\ 2 \\ 1 \end{matrix}$ ——— so as not to confuse students when

you say, "The first line is E (treble clef)."

C) Reading notation backwards, right to left as well as forwards, in both rhythmic and melodic lines, not only increases the reading facility and is fun to try, but in many cases helps to correct reading reversals. Experiencing a deliberate reversal establishes what a reversal is; and this helps children to overcome the problem.

D) Peripheral reading of rhythmic notation involves eye tracking in many directions and is good exercise for facility. Place several examples on the board:

1.
2.
3.
4.

* Contributed by Jeanne Loudon, Music Specialist, Winchester, Mass.

Directions:

a) Speak and clap each phrase above.

b) Volunteers in turn clap one of the above phrases (no speaking). Class members designate which phrase it was by raising one, two or three, etc. fingers.

c) Ask for volunteer to clap #12 (1 and 2); #31 (3 and 1).

d) Students in turn call out a 3-digit number (413) for volunteers to clap; a 4-digit number, etc. (The object is to connect the phrases smoothly without pausing or losing a beat.)

E) Sight reading games using body percussion

Class selects a different sound (clap, snap, etc.) for each note value to be used.

Example: ♩ = clap; ♪ = foot tap; o = snap; ⊓ = leg pat.

(rest)

Perform it in two part canon, the second part beginning the line one measure after the first part. Perform it with one section reading it left to right, the other right to left.

F) Using hand percussion instruments in performance

Select several hand percussions to perform the above rhythmic line in canon, each instrument beginning one measure apart.

Each instrument performs only one kind of note. Four players perform the above line.

Add a half note ostinato on two timpani and clap the rhythmic line against the ostinato.

G) Memory Games

After clapping and speaking a given rhythmic line such as above in Ta's and Tee's, erase one measure. Repeat the total line, clapping. Erase a second measure and repeat the entire line. Continue until the measures are all erased and the line is memorized.

Walk the beat and clap the memorized line, moving freely, not in a circle, but turning, changing directions without bumping anyone. Stopping for four beats before repeating the line. Changing space levels of the clapping on each phrase such as, overhead, side, behind, etc. can be added to the rules.

H) Flash cards for reading games

Make different combinations of either rhythmic note values and rests, or *so-fa* syllables and rests (pulse or beat phrases without rhythmic content). Place along chalk tray or scatter on the floor for a circle game.

1) Use suggestions in *F*.

2) Add a clapping ostinato and speak in Ta's and Tee's the rhythmic phrases.

3) Two players, one on each timpani or with contrasting percussion, alternate the measures.

To develop "reading ahead," a row of students, each holding one flash card, faces the class. Each card holder turns his card down as the class reaches that measure, thus requiring the readers to look ahead at the measure beyond the one they are clapping.

I) Extending notation with hand percussion

1) Example: | | ⊓ | Four students (triangle, claves, maracas and hand drum) perform the given phrase, facing the class. (Maracas play the eighth notes). After several repetitions of the phrase, class closes eyes while players rearrange themselves. (Maracas takes a different position) | ⊓ | | Class then reads and claps the new organization, adding it to their first pattern: | | ⊓ |, | ⊓ | |

Players again change their order and class adds the new pattern to their previous ones. When the four possibilities have been found, the class tries to say the alphabet with their clapping of the entire four patterns, giving one letter to each clapping sound. This game can also be used for dictation practice.

2) Syncopation: Using the example above, | | ⊓ |, ask for five players, two for the maracas. This time the two maracas players must put one quarter-note player between them: | ♭| ♭| Class reads and claps the phrase, adding the new possibilities as they are found; | ♭| ♭|, | | ♭| ♭, ♭| ♭| | :‖

J) Adding melody to a rhythmic line | | ⊓ | etc.
S M S L S

1) Using a given number of syllables, the five tone pentatonic scale for example (L S M R D), and starting on *so,* pass the tune around the class for each to contribute his choice of syllables, one per person, until the tune is completed. Class sings the line, makes desired changes and sings it again.

2) Add an ostinato accompaniment on the tonebar instruments such as a bordun

pattern on 5ths:  All sing the melody.

3) Sing it in two voice canon.

4) Try singing the melody backwards, right to left, and decide preference; or use the tune both ways, one against the other, or one after the other, making a longer piece.

K) Rhythmic notation with color cardboards

Using a different color for each note value, cut strips according to size relationship of the note values. Example:

$$\text{Red} = \mathbf{o} \text{ ; whole card}$$
$$\text{Green} = \text{\textomega} \text{ ; half card}$$
$$\text{Blue} = \text{♩} \text{ ; one fourth card}$$
$$\text{Yellow} = \text{♪} \text{ ; one eighth card}$$

Set up a mystery melody on the chalk try, such as *Hot Cross Buns.*

$$|\ |\ \square,\ \ |\ |\ \square,\ \ ||||||||,\ \ |\ |\ \square.$$

Play the line with hand percussion instruments; in canon; backwards. Ask for volunteers to change or rearrange each measure into a new rhythm line, borrowing, exchanging cards as they wish. Class performs the new line, and perhaps gives it a new melody, using the same syllables.

L) Dictation games

Begin with short phrases:

1) Leader claps the phrase: | ⊓ | |
2) Class echo claps the phrase: | ⊓ | |
3) Class speaks the phrase in Ta's and Tee's: "Ta Tee Tee Ta Ta"
4) Class writes the phrase: | ⊓ | |

For clarity, follow these four steps consistently. Students should write the phrases across the paper rather than in vertical order, placing a comma to separate the phrases. Later, measure bars can be used.

Rests or silent beats are indicated by a gesture or a finger snap.

M) Changing the pulse unit and meters for flexibility

Use different note values, ♪, ♩ for the pulse unit, changing frequently. Mix and combine flashcards in $\frac{4}{♩}, \frac{5}{♩}, \frac{3}{♪}$ meters.

N) Melodic dictation games

Begin with short phrases in pulse or beat only, not in rhythmic line. Leader makes hand signals, silently indicating the tone sequence: S L S M S

Class echoes, singing the phrase with the hand signals: S L S M S

Class writes the phrase in syllables: S L S M S   After several phrases, ask for volunteers to sing the entire melody line. Sing the line L. to R.

Extensions:

Add rhythmic content to the syllables: S L S M S

Leader signals a mystery tune with silent hand signs; class identifies

Leader signals a mystery tune, making one wrong syllable; class corrects

Leader signals one phrase to be answered by a volunteer using the same tones but

in a different order: (S L L S M) (S M S L L)

O) Rhythmic problems:

The foremost problem encountered in instrumental and choral groups is rhythm. *Rhythmic expression has its source in speech.* Therefore speech clarifies rhythm and can be used again and again to solve ensemble problems. Practice in finding beat, accents rests or pauses in rhythmic sayings and rhymes, helps the student to solve some of his own rhythmic problems. To understand and perform more complex rhythms, break down the entire phrase into the smallest denominator or note value in the phrase:

| ♩♪ | = ♫♫♫ ♫♫♫ ♫♫♫ = "ti-ri ti-ri, ti-ri, ti-ri, ti-ri, ti-ri"

NOTATION IN THE MIDDLE SCHOOL

With older students, the basics of notation are still needed but they can be introduced differently.

Suggestions: Using the same straight line to denote a quarter beat, begin with a proverb, such as, "Taking pride / / in what you do / / is a sign / / of maturity. /" These inserted beats or pauses can be played on the timpani with the speaking which is then transferred to the tonebar instruments for improvisation in melody. For example, set up the

instruments in F pentatonic, and the timpani in (F) and (C). Each player in turn improvises

his own melody based on the text (every syllable), while the timpanist plays the inserted beats:

* Xylophone

* Example from 7th grade, Kino Junior High, Mesa, Ariz. Patricia Terry, Music Instructor

After the proverb, take up the spelling of the days of the week, pronouncing

"Cap-i-tal S (-U,-N, etc.) on the timpani and showing the written and spoken sym-

bols for the triplet figure: tri-ple-ty Ta. Practice it with leg pat and speech, ex-

plaining that it is like a "3 for 1" sale, or three for a quarter "special." "Wash-ing-ton,

George," is another speech pattern for this rhythm. Although the eighth note symbol

has already been used in speech patterns, "See you lat-er al-li-ga-tor," and, "Travel

teaches tol-er-a-tion," the speech term of "Tee tee" would seem silly and

babyish. An alternative to this is found within the "triplety" term, with the explanation

that the last syllable, "ty" is used for the division of "2 for 1," "Ty-ty Ta." The three

patterns, "Wash-ing-ton, Mar-tha, George," can be tried on the timpani and other
instruments and written in different sequences for performance:

To express the half note in speech, simply swallow the second "Ta" and you have,
"Ta-ah" duration. Similarly for the dotted half note and whole note durations:

$$\quad \text{Ta - ah} \qquad\qquad \text{Ta-ah-ah, Ta-ah-ah-ah.}$$

One teacher* has good results with the ♩. and ♩. by having the students actually
dot the note in the air for emphasis and understanding. Feeling or even "bumping" the
added dot helps to clarify its value and duration. *Children learn by their "feelings." Before
they can internalize a beat or rhythm, they must be able to externalize it with speech and
muscular expression.*

* Caroline Ostrander, Music Specialist, Ithaca, N.Y.

$\frac{6}{8}\left(\frac{6}{8}\right)$ Use the count of 6 as the speech base: 1, 2, 3, 4, 5, 6.

1) Clap to the left side on 1; to the right on 4; timpani plays on 1 and 6. Everyone counts and walks the six beats, adding the clapped 1 and 4.

Sequence: 1 2 3 4 5 6 :‖
         >   >

2) Half of the group claps on 1, 3 and 5: 1 2 3 4 5 6. Take away the counting
                                          >   >   >
aloud and think the numbers while clapping and walking.

3) Try the same plan with percussion instruments instead of clapping.

4) Each person chooses his own two or three numbers out of the six for clapping. (No walking.) Timpani starts the ensemble. Others join.

Such an ensemble can be charted for percussion or "found" sound which will accompany improvisations by the tonebar instruments.

A swing beat can be expressed in a six unit with accents on 1 2 3 4 5 6
                                                              >   >>   >

A six meter can have ♪, ♩, or ♩. as the unit value.

Try other meters such as, 5 7 8 or 9, charting them before transferring to the five-
                          ♩ ♩ ♪ ♪
line staff reading.

With dotted quarters or half notes, pulse the ♩. with three eighths, in clapping or with the hand signal so the number of eighths in a ♩. is expressed. If the dotted note is followed by an eighth, accent it slightly for clarity. ♫♩ ♪ ♪
                                                                          >   >

Extend rhythmic reading into a two- and three-line score:

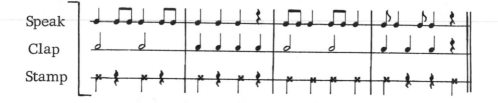

Perform only two lines first, then three. This is difficult.

For added challenge, try clapping the top line and speaking the second line.

ATONAL SIGHT READING*

Introduce atonal reading by using *so-fa* syllables with movable *do.* Looking for relationships in tonal patterns is a natural path to atonal reading.

* Atonal music has no preset key signature, nor home tone.

Preparation: Example

1) What other relationships does each phrase contain?

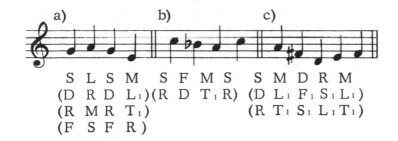

```
    S  L S M    S  F M S    S M D R M
   (D  R D L₁) (R  D T₁ R) (D L₁ F₁ S₁ L₁)
   (R  M R T₁)             (R T₁ S₁ L₁ T₁)
   (F  S F R )
```

2) Sing with hand signals and *so-fa* syllables:

```
S  L  S  M→D  R  M  S→M  F  R  M D→S→M  R  D  D⁴→S  F  M
```

The arrows indicate a changing relationship in the melody.

3) How would you sing the melody below in the key of F Major? How would you sing it atonally? How many different ways are there? Can you change the relationship or syllable patterns on each measure?

LATIN AMERICAN RHYTHMS

In Latin American music there is a sophistication beyond the straight metered measure and vertical beats into an "over-the-bar" phrase, especially the Bossa Nova rhythm. Based on 8 in 4 time signature, the accents are on 1 2 3 4 5 6 7 8, 1 - 2 - 3 - 4; a two-measure phrase. These changing accents immediately open the framework into flexible and freer expression, rhythmic and melodic. Again, by using speech and number patterns to delineate the accents and flow, students quickly grasp the content and become able performers and readers. (See Chapter I, Perspectives; Chapter II, Coordination.)

There are many kinds of notation* besides the traditional which should be explored by

* See Bibliography, (Music) for Murray Shafer's books and "Experimental Sound in the Classroom" by Brian Dennis

students. Try team and group projects in composition based on story ideas that are projected on large sheets of wrapping paper with one horizontal line for each sound or instrument in the ensemble. Colors, pictures and symbols can be used, with the performers being responsible for the interpretation of their own notation. Rhythmic or arhythmic symbols can be used.

Aleatory (or chance) music can be drawn from many sources. (See *Today With Music,* page 39).

Graphs, boxes and descriptive drawings plus notation designed by the students themselves. (See *Today With Music,* page 3.)

CONCLUSION

The student's oral abilities in language are usually quite far ahead of his spelling and written language abilities. What he expresses in speech should and can be transferred into his hands, mallets and into drum playing. His rhythmic oral and muscular expression should precede written symbols, and prepare him for written notation, just as the *so-fa* syllables and hand signals lead into staff reading. *If the student is too tense to read notation (language or music) give him more music-making and rhythmic expression in movement.* This is the warning that often goes unheeded in the teacher's rush to produce reading skills.

CHAPTER 7

Movement

A generation ago when man finished his day's work he needed rest; today he needs exercise.

. . . . and knowing man's need of comfort, God gave him music . . . . *Anon.*

This chapter contains material for teachers and trainees who wish to understand the basic principles of movement. It is based on the work of the late Rudolf Laban of England, his exponents and others.

To explore the how, why, what, and where of movement is in itself a complex task without having to listen to music at the same time.Therefore, few recordings or piano compositions are mentioned. For rhythmic expression, use music that is composed or performed by the teacher or students themselves. Such music is more purposeful and goes naturally with their singing from the first day of school.

INTRODUCTION

Q. Why is movement needed in the classroom?
A. 1) Because movement is a vehicle for all expression.

2) To counterbalance the neglected use of the child's body in today's environment. Too many of the leisure hours are spent in TV watching and spectator non-involvement.

Dance forms of past civilizations have been closely related to work habits, beliefs and political life. With the industrial age came the need to discard the heavy costumes and court head-dresses to accord freedom of movement in expressing human feelings, passions and spiritual beliefs. The mechanized age brought with it the need for release and expression of soul—a flowing lyrical style of dance and sense of poetry in movement. This style was a counterbalance to the work habits of man which no longer engaged the entire body. The loss of needed communication with nature also indicated that man must somehow compensate for these unfulfilled needs during his leisure hours.

With children, it is their leisure hours that have had damaging effects. Their 3,000 hours of T.V. watching (260 days of sitting) expended before kindergarten, build up a hypertension. For many children, this amounts to a state of mental ill health by the time they enter school.

While this problem is not being dealt with in many teacher training courses, the primary task of education has now become one of restoring mental health! A child's out-of-school hours have become almost sterile with inactivity, very little language interaction, little play or investigation, all of which are vitally essential to a child's normal growth. Movement is as necessary to mental and physical development as food. Classroom hours must somehow contain and provide these unfulfilled needs. Putting children into desks with a "sit-still" command only furthers their already hypertensive condition. Nor will aimless wandering and permissive looseness help them. We must somehow restore the child's lost media of play but in a larger dimension and scope.

Let us consider the premise that dance is the basic art of man.

"In the beginning man danced by himself—random movements. Then by repeating the rhythmic movements he gained a feeling of ecstasy as well as a supernatural state of mind and emotion. When he repeated his dance, he recreated that feeling of magic power. In later development he acquired group feeling and became involved in group dancing using geometric patterns, closed circle, open semi-circle, parallel lines or a winding line, etc.

"Primitive magic dances became religious ceremonies and later grew into Greek dances. With mind development dance became more restrained and complex in form but was still rich in meaning."[1]

Movement is not only essential to man, it is also one of his most powerful means of self expression, communication and outlet for well-being. It is a balance wheel for his emotional equilibrium. Rhythm and melody express movement, and movement is the natural human response to music. Therefore, the direct and natural path for the child's understanding of music and musical form, and his development of musicality, muscular coordination and freedom of self-expression, lies in movement. If he moves with the musical phrase, *expresses* the rhythmic pattern with his body instruments, he consequently feels it and understands it.

What a child expresses in direction and movement, he can express and translate into other media. The more able he becomes in flow of movement and coordination, the more flexible he becomes in adapting and controlling his movements according to environmental changes.

There are different effort elements (weight, space, time and flow) in movement which vary according to man's different attitudes, reasons, purpose and intent. Children become aware of these elements through a deliberate experiencing of these motion factors. A child's discovery of his body potential, is essential to his developing knowledgeable control and direction of movement. This is done through problem solving games utilizing opposites in each of these above elements and their various combinations.

Specifics in directions and boundaries are just as important in motion development for children as specifics in academic learning. Rather than aimless walking, running or marching, there should be a focus of attention and direction in each movement. Consider these examples:

[1]By special permission from Master's Thesis on History of the Development of Orff Schulwerk in the United States by Janice Rapley (Soderberg) 1969.

1) Leading the whole movement with one part of the body—a small part such as a hand, elbow, shoulder, eyebrow.

2) Introducing opposites in time, weight and space such as:

—Tiptoe quickly to the door

—Glide through mud carrying a hundred-pound stone

—Ripple one finger and let the ripple travel through the entire body like an echo chamber

  —then freeze!

3) Specific imagery: "Be a candle, slim and tall, slowly melting, dripping, fall."

4) Characterization.

Dealing with opposites in the elements of motion helps children to:

   a) discover what their bodies can do

   b) direct their movements

   c) control their movements

   d) understand concepts of slow-fast, tension-relaxation, strong-weak, heavy-light, expansion-contraction, closed-open, flow-motionless, in-out, straight-twisted, up-down, and in combinations, using time, space, weight together.[2]

In essence, our premise is to help a child develop skills and control-flow through a focused movement based upon his own way of moving—a personality and self-image growth through movement.

We are living in a space-conscious age, yet with an ever-decreasing amount of space. Techniques toward economy of motion as well as direction or focus must be considered in our guidance with children.

A child deprived of movement becomes a retarded child. Consider therefore how important to children's future well-being is a "rich movement—life."

LABAN'S LARGE GOALS

1) To guide children's natural urge to do dance-like movements into a linear flow of movement and an understanding of the principles governing movement.

2) To preserve their spontaneity into adult life.

3) To encourage their creative expression and combine it with intellectual knowledge.

Children are mainly concerned with speed and strong, straight, or direct movements. They begin their lives in a horizontal relationship to their environment. Vertical, upright position comes later. A basic need, even to adulthood, is re-experiencing this horizontal relationship. Movement on the floor, sitting and lying, is important and needed. To develop flow with these natural movements, they need first to explore and use *space* imaginatively. Awareness of narrowness and width, of places around them, above, below, and points between.

AWARENESS OF SPACE

A) From a given stance, stretch to every point of space surrounding the body with arms, elbows, head, shoulders, legs, etc. This perimeter represents your personal spatial sphere.

[2] These ideas and directions in movement education were inspired primarily by the work of Rudolf Laban and his exponents, Ann Driver, Rachel Percival, and Vera Gray of England.

81

B) "Tuning up" (1) Shake out different parts of the body while staying within this personal sphere. (2) Contract (stiffen) and relax. Loosen separate parts of the body in slow motion and in normal to fast motion. Use hands, head, tongue, shoulders, chin, feet, hips, knees, entire body. The tongue is an important muscle that effects and reflects both tension and relaxation in other parts of the body; for example, relax the tongue; do you feel your entire body relaxing? When a student is writing for example, and his tongue is twisting and turning at the side of his mouth, ask him to steer the pencil with his tongue (imaginary) and the result is a freeing of the pencil tension.

C) Transfer the personal sphere into a new space, i.e. by taking one's own space to a new location with walking motion, running, skipping, swaying. Find out what is required in good walking, good swaying, good running, and in good arm movement. What about head and neck movements?

Express suppleness with these specific effort-actions:

1) Walk to a new place, stretching to the clouds . . . . . relax.
2) Lie down and with your feet, walk on the ceiling . . . . . relax.
3) With one foot, turn a screw into the ground . . . . . relax.
4) Skip along the beach in sand . . . . . relax.
5) Flick away specks of dust in front, above, behind, below . . . . . relax.
6) Sink to the floor without any jerks, rise quickly . . . . . relax.

Try all actions in reverse . . . . . a playback.

7) Do a crab walk.
8) Do a broken down bronco walk.

Conclusion: Suppleness of movement is important to development of linear flow. It is made up of contraction and relaxation in muscular rhythmic action.

To help students experience the element of flow, try a sequence of movements that are continuous and become longer. For example, starting with fingers, add wrists, the whole hand, in a continuing motion that widens and lengthens in space as elbows, shoulders, upper body, and finally entire body become involved . . . . . relax. Explore space with hands; explore what your hands and fingers can do.

While lying down, begin a motion with only the toes. Add heels, ankles, foot, legs, knees, hips (twist or roll over) . . . . . relax. How much of this can be done standing?

While standing, what parts of the body move well together? Try elbows and knees, hips and shoulders, feet and hands, and head and chin.

Conclusion: Use separately and combine small muscle movements and large muscle movements. Use specifics in directions and boundaries, yet with an element of choice.

BASIC DESIGNS IN MOVEMENT

Straight line:

Curve, circle:

Twisted pattern:

Angle:

Problems:

1) Draw these shapes using different parts of the body: finger, hand, elbow, head, foot, toe, hips, shoulders, etc., in different space zones and positions (lying, sitting, kneeling).

2) In a continuous successive order, use different parts of the body to draw a given design.

3) Use the whole body. Lead the movement with one part and make jet trails with these patterns. (linear flow of movement)

Conclusion: Direct experience in drawing the four basic patterns of movement, first with different parts of the body, then successively in a sequence, and finally using the whole body will develop further awareness, control and understanding of movement.

EXPRESSING OPPOSITES

In every session for movement development, make use of opposites. Use the entire body or different parts thereof.

1) Tension—relaxation (squirm/motionless; wiggle/stop; etc.)
2) Time—(slow/fast; walk/run; etc.)
3) Space—(out/in; up/down; narrow/wide; over/under; etc.)
4) Weight—(heavy/light; strong/weak; etc.)
5) Flow—(sudden stop from sustained flow using above opposites)

Use a sound signal from a drum or triangle for stopping. . . . run . . . stop!; glide . . . freeze!

Conclusion: Experiencing opposites in movement will clarify the meaning of each.

EXPLORING SPACE USING OPPOSITES AND DESIGNS

Directions: Reach out to every point possible in space from where you stand. *Where* is the *shortest* distance you can reach away from yourself? The farthest distance? Stand on one foot and reach out using available parts of your body, even turning your body. Does this give more extension to your spatial sphere?

1) Expanding and contracting: fingers; one arm; both arms; one foot; both feet; legs; elbows; mouth; eyes; chest; entire body; etc.

2) Raising and lowering: entire body, upper part of body, shoulders, elbows, arms, one leg, eyes, head, both heels, etc.

3) Up and around; under and over: different parts of your body, etc. Carry a heavy sack of meal; give it to another person.

4) Push heavy space objects away from you in all directions with open palms of hands, with elbows, shoulders, head, feet, etc. (sustained, heavy movements).

5) Shoot arrows or small objects into space with elbows, toes, nose, top of head, hands, knees, etc.

Try the problems above in rhythmic patterns of equal length for the contrasting actions. Use different percussion instruments to accompany. (Wood sounds for staccato movements; cymbal or gong for sustained flow)

Direction: Moving to a new space.

Preparation: Make a list on the board of action words that you can do in your own spaces such as: rise, drop, curl, twist, jump, shake, spring, stretch, pull, push, dab, press, wring, punch, slash, straighten, tighten, flop, hang, slump, etc.

Problem: "Do Not Bump"*

A) Decide on a new spot in the room. Don't tell anyone.

B) Select one of the words from your list above and use this as the theme for taking your space to a new location.

C) Decide what part of your body will lead the whole movement, then go to your new place using your chosen action word as your guide.

D) Return to your original place via a different route, moving backwards and leading the action with a different part of your body. There are countless action words which can be carried out in the personal sphere. Many can also be used to take ones' personal sphere elsewhere through focus of one part of the body leading the entire movement.

Conclusion: Focus of movement enables us to find out how and what our bodies can do.

LABAN'S BASIC EFFORTS IN MOVEMENT

1. *Wringing* (flexible, sustained, firm)
   (Variations: twisting, stretching, pulling, squeezing)
   Hands (wring out clothes), arms, legs, shoulders, knees, whole body with a pulling, twisting strength. Try kneeling position; sitting; lying.

2. *Pressing* (firm, direct and sustained)
   (Variations: pushing, pulling, hitting)
   Hands with palms out; with arms; shoulders, legs, etc.

3. *Glide* (sustained, light, direct)
   (Variations: swaying, swinging, smearing)
   Palms of hands move across smooth surface in all direction; one foot slides over floor; body bows, sways; combine gliding steps with gliding motions of hands, arms, shoulders, etc. Try motions in kneeling position; sitting; lying.

4. *Float* (sustained, flexible, light)
   (Variations: flying, stirring, drifting, stroking)
   Imagine fog; smoke, clouds. Use arms; shoulders; knees; head; feet; legs; away from body and toward body; also kneeling; sitting; lying positions. "Stir a thick broth."

5. *Flicking* (light, flexible, sudden)
   (Variations: flapping, jerking flicks, flipping)
   Flick a feather with hands, elbows, foot, knees, shoulders; away from body, behind, over, etc.

6. *Slash* (sudden, firm, flexible)
   (Variations: whipping, beating, throwing)
   Legs slash as in jumping. Try each arm striking high and downward, outward— all zones. Each leg slashes; shoulders, elbows, knees, feet, hands, etc.

7. *Punch* (sudden, direct, firm)
   (Variations: thrusting, shoving, piercing)
   Feel strength in whole body. Extending behind, over and in deep zones of action with hands; elbows; knees; feet; also kneeling, sitting, lying; slow motion; arms crossed.

8. *Dab* (direct, sudden, light)
   (Variations: patting, tapping, shaking dabs)
   Use all directions, light, quick; hands; feet; shoulders, knees, head; with crossed arms; etc.

In addition to the eight basic efforts there are action verbs that exaggerate different basic effort actions such as: smashing, groping, dragging, etc. There are also one-element actions such as: falling, rising, etc. Any of these actions may occur in time and space with weight and flow.

Exploring Space grows with time and weight elements in a continuity of movement.

"Making a statue" is the opposite of movement and belongs with each development of movement, ending that movement.

Contrasts can be drawn with partners:

1) Making and changing statue shapes—expressing differences between large and small, tall and short, wide and narrow statues.

2) Expressing contrasts in movement (response). One moves, the other responds (straight, twisting, forwards, backwards).

3) Contrasts in speed (quick—slow).

Arms and legs as tools/instruments

Use the hands and arms as tools for gripping, pinching, dipping, scooping, scattering, plucking, writing in the air, sawing wood, hammering, chopping, ball pitching, picking apples, picking up stones, rowing, etc.

Besides stepping, leaping, turning, running, etc., use the feet for gathering leaves, strewing pebbles, making a channel, tossing sand, etc., with alternating feet as bicycling.

Combine arms and legs in floor-touch walking; somersaults; making a table; bowling; pole vaulting; crab walking, elephant walk; etc.

Actions leaving the ground

After exploring different ways and directions of walking, running, etc., consider springing actions: strong elastic thrust that is felt in the legs just before leaving the ground in a leap. Explore skipping and jumping as well. By keeping the upper part of the body relaxed, the take-off is easier and elastic strength for action can be felt and focused in the legs. Try turning leaps, skipping, jumping sideways, etc.

Game

EXAMPLES:

1) "Jack be nimble, Jack be quick,
   Jack jump over the candlestick,

Jack jump high;
Jack jump low;
Jumping sideways, off he goes.''
Try the same verse with *skipping*:
"skips by the candlestick.''

and with leaping.

2) Hula hoops laid in a line and spaced for leaps, jumps or skips. Drum keeps a rhythmic beat as one by one goes down the course. Aim is not to touch the hoops. Keep a continuous flowing movement.

Review sitting and kneeling actions that do not involve leaving the floor. Notice the contrast in intensity of elevation required for leaping movements.

Group movement

Problem: How to move like one body.

A) By specifics in: a) leading the motion with same designated part of body. b) establishing a group center, leader and direction. c) Watching successive groups; evaluating. One group moves; another group responds with counter moves watching exact distances and space ratios. d) group formations: row; half circle; circle; cluster; angles.

B) Group practice:

1) Rising as one body.
2) Sinking.
3) Leaning outward, inward; stretching upward or outward, recoiling.
4) Row or line: without changing location, stretch row from center.
5) Moving one foot, lengthen row by growing from one end.
6) Moving one foot, lengthen row by growing from both ends.
7) Run in a straight direction—follow leader.
8) Run in a curving line that turns into a circle.
9) Make the circle into a row again.

Problem: Each group selects one of the eight Basic Efforts to carry out in a sustained flow. Start in a row and end in a different shape or formation. Lead the movement and effort with one part of body. Each group performs as others watch and evaluate.

Exercises to try:

1) (a) Make dabbing motions while speaking a rhyme or the alphabet.
   (b) Make wringing movements with rhyme or alphabet.

   What are the differences in voice tone and facial expressions between (a) and (b)? In feelings portrayed?

2) (a) Make pressing motions while speaking verse (pushing away from).
   (b) Make floating motions while speaking.

   Compare attitudes expressed.

3) (a) Express anger with the elbows; feet; hands; etc.
   (b) Express delight with the elbows; feet; hands; etc.

What are the differences? Name the basic effort used in each.

4) (a) Express fear with the whole body.
   (b) Express sudden fear with only the breathing.

   Is relaxation or contraction (tension) dominant?

5) (a) Express tenderness, compassion with arm motions.
   (b) Express shutting out or turning off—refusal to listen.

   What are the attitudes in (a) and (b)? Effort actions in each? Movement elements in each? Time-weight and Space-flow?

Movement in relation to nature

Observe movement in lightning, rain, wind, snow, streams, waves, clouds, surf, tornado funnel, etc. Describe the movements and try them in terms of the eight basic efforts, and opposites in space, time and weight, directions and shapes to clarify understanding of the principles of human movement.

Movement in relationship to sound

Explore:
   1) Contrasting textures of sound. Spreading or sustaining as against staccato, dry, sudden. (metal versus wood)
   2) Contrasting dynamics of sound. Louder as against softer.
   3) Contrasting registers. Deep or low sound as against high sound.

Movement In relation to rhythmic content

Use walking to running; skipping to leaping; sudden stops; gradual stops; different levels and directions in space; separate parts of body according to the rhythmic qualities and tempos.
   Recordings:
Bizet; *Les Chevaux de Bois*, from *Jeux d'Enfants*

Brahms: *Hungarian Dance No. 6*

Dvorak: *Slavonic Dance No. 2*

Moussorgsky: *Pictures from an Exhibition*

Movement in relation to melody

Express melody in flow of movement of phrase—by changing directions; by hesitating; lifting; changing levels and/or kind of motion; and weight.
   Recordings:
Schubert: *German Dance Op. 33, No. 7*

R. Strauss: *Waltz—from Der Rosenkavalier*

Movement in relation to musical form

FORM: Canon, Rondo, Theme and Variations, etc.
- A) Canon:
  1) Begin with echoing phrases of movement since canon is based on imitation.
  2) Rhythmic imitation of simple movements.
  3) Extend the phrase so the echo imitation overlaps.
  4) Use a familiar song canon such as *"Frère Jacques"* to develop movement in canon: Students form a square—sides A, B, C, and D.

First Phrase: | | | | | | | | | |

Lines A and C move 4 steps toward center and 4 steps back.
Lead off with right foot.

Second Phrase: | | ♩ | | | ♩ |

Lines A and C turn to right, take 3 steps forward and 3 back.

Third Phrase: ⊓ ⊓ | | | ⊓ ⊓ | | |

Stand in place and do leg pat l. r., in rhythm.

Fourth Phrase: | | ♩ | | | ♩ |

Stand in place and clap hands on first measure, slap leg
right, left, right on second measure.

PART II: Lines B and D begin *their* part of song and action when lines A and C are starting the 2nd phrase. Lines B and D carry out the same actions as A and C have finished (one phrase behind).
- B) Rondo: A—B—A—C—A

The first and oft repeated *A* section is usually a learned set of movements, while *B, C,* sections etc. are improvised and often done by individuals or small groups in contrast to the larger group performance—*A.*

EXAMPLE: "All Night, All Day".* Song and circle movement can be Section *A.* Improvised, away-from-the-circle movements can be done between repeats of the song.

Theme and variations: Again, this can be a learned set of movements for the *theme,* with improvised or practiced individual or group variations based on the learned theme.
EXAMPLE: A Country and Western song. Different partners step into the ring to dance, each couple doing their own variations of the song rhythm.

Movement in relation to other cultures and countries (See Chapter on Rhythmic Coordination)

Conclusion: It is said that movement is the essence of life—that without movement there is atrophy and death!

Daily attention to this life-need rests not only on the physical education instructor and music specialist but also on the classroom teacher, the principal and every member of the Board of Education!

> ". . . . every child has a right to know how to achieve control of his body in order that he may use it (with economy) and to the limit of his ability for the expression of his own reactions to life."
>
> Margaret H. Doubler
> from *Dance: A Creative Art Experience*

SUMMARY: Daily Movement for Personality and Total Growth.

1) Develop awareness: a) leading a movement with one part of the body; fingers, hand, wrist, head, shoulder, hip, knee, toe, foot, etc. b) use specifics in directions and focus.

2) Involve large muscles and small muscles. Large, vigorous movements and small, light movements.

3) Bring feelings (actual movement) and knowledge of movement together by considering:

   a) where to move—fundamental directions.

   b) how to move there—

   c) what moves to get there—what part of the body leads the movement and what kind of movement takes place.

   d) how else could it be done? What else could be done? Where else could one move?

4) Express opposites and variation in time, weight, space and flow.

5) Form different designs and shapes, singly and in group formations.

6) (a) realize extent of movement expression within personal sphere.

   (b) extend this body sphere into general sphere using different locomotions and basic efforts.

7) At all times reach towards *more linear flow of movement.*

CHAPTER 8

Awareness and Sensitivity

Let us "see, hear and touch with the same awareness
we hope to foster in young people."
—From speech by Lloyd Alexander to Ace One and
Children's Book Council)

"Nothing can be done without awareness. With it, anything is possible."

—Martin Buber

Sound makes the first track to the brain and brings with it a natural response in movement. It therefore holds tremendous potential for development of either sensitivity or insensitivity, awareness or dullness.

INFANCY

The newborn infant receives his first information about his environment through sound. The mother's voice is a comforting melody to his ears and he responds in movement. The father's voice, the sounds made by other members of the family, the songs of birds, streams, bells, or chimes will also be heard, each bearing information and significance. A harsh, raucous sound, such as a door banging, a scolding voice, or a child's scream, will occasion an immediate response of withdrawal.

Should the offending sounds continue, his response becomes dulled or turned off; the track to the brain slows or ceases. If there are many such sounds going on, the emotional distress may be evident in crying, nervousness, jerky movements and random flinging of arms and legs. *Rhythmic sound* and *tonal sound* usually bring favorable movement response and well-being. Unceasing noise (unwanted or undesirable sound) and high decibels of sound can have a damaging effect on his entire system. Sound pollution is increasing over much of the nation, dulling the senses and awareness.

CHILDHOOD

By the time children enter school many have developed a skill for closing out and turning off uninteresting and disturbing sounds. Others are insensitive to sound in general, unresponsive and apathetic. Still others are hypertense and hyperactive, unable to concentrate, and have short attention spans. (With these last two, there are usually other contributing factors.)

A. Restoring and/or developing sensitivity to sound begins with awareness of its existence—not with many sounds simultaneously, but with *one* sound—or perhaps better, silence! Induce and stir the listening powers with problem-solving experiments. Because creativity and imagination are linked together and develop with awareness and sensitivity, whatever stimulates one is affecting the others.

1) How long does a sound last?

EXPERIMENT: A cymbal is held by the handle by one person blindfolded. Another person quietly strikes the cymbal with a mallet. Everyone listens. When the sound can no longer be heard, each person raises his hand. (Blindfolded person will be the last one to raise his hand.)

Q.   Why did *he* hear the sound so much longer?

A.   a) He was closer to the cymbal.

b) Ask the student who held the cymbal. He may thoughtfully say that he *felt* the sound in his arm muscles, which is correct.

2) Can we hear sound with any other part of the body? (Muscles of arms, legs, face, etc.) Can you SEE sound?

EXPERIMENT: Place grains of sawdust, sand or salt on the top of the cymbal. Watch what happens when the cymbal is tapped. Did you see sound? Where else could you see sound?

3) Experiment with textures of sound.

   a) A cymbal is what texture? (metal)

   b) Look around the room for possible metal sounds. Catalog them in your memory. Do not tell anyone.

   c) Another texture: (wood) Look around for different wood textures. Don't tell.

   d) Any other textures in the room? (skin, plastic, glass, etc.)

PROBLEM: Form three teams. Each team selects a leader.

Team I will use all wood sounds and prepare a sequence based on this pattern:

Team II takes all metal sounds and makes a sequence based on this pattern:

Team III takes all the other textures found and builds a sequence on this pattern:

Composition with textures

Allow four or five minutes for preparation and arrange players in the order desired. Each person plays his part in turn, without breaking the continuity. Everyone listens. NOTE: Do not use live human sounds—the skin refers to a possible drumhead.

Development of a composition begins with alternating and combining categories. Everyone tries the three sequences above with:

(metal)   (wood)   (misc.)

Could a new sound be added to perform the rests? Perhaps one human sound of "clap." Select volunteers to clap the rests. Leaders of each team will select one of their sound textures and be ready to perform. Extend the composition to three or more players— one from each team with their respective categories. Now another three players. Each set of three will need an additional player to do their rests, which could be snap, stamp, or leg-pat, overlapping the three parts. Example: Part I begins. II enters after 1 measure, and so on.

Player: (1)   (2)   (3)

Metal:

Wood:

Misc.:

Tape the composition and listen to it for evaluation. Perhaps someone could add a melody by improvising on the xylophone (wood); glockenspiel (metal).
ASSIGNMENT: Look around for new sounds of metal, wood, etc., in your house and on the way to school.   4) Awareness of inconsequential (?) sounds.
Q. Can you remember the first sounds you heard when you awoke today: List them and remember them.
Q. The last sounds before you went to sleep? Listen tonight and report tomorrow morning.
    5) Other sounds around us.
    a) Q. What are some of the sounds in this room that we do not pay attention to? (fan, pencil sharpener, feet, etc.) At home? . . . On the street? . . . On the playground?
    b) Are there sounds in the ground? Have you ever put your ear to the ground in spring—fall, winter, summer? Under the ocean? In a shell?
    c) Is there sound in a stone? Tap a stone with different tools and see if there is a difference in the sounds?
    d) What about human sounds? (Other than word language: mouth, feet, hands)
    1) Take partners and quickly build a duet based on mouth sounds only. Present them to the class.
    2) Partners again. This time a duet between hands and feet. One partner uses hands, the other uses feet. Present the duets to the class.
    Notice how many shades in dynamics (loud or soft) are possible with hands. For example, from leg-slap, shoulder, elbow, arm, finger, and wrist. How many sounds are possible with the feet, from tiptoe to heels, to stairs, to different kinds of floors, from bare feet to socks to shoes? These sounds are among those we take for granted. In the next days listen for other such sounds.
    6) Exploring shades of sounds in a single object or instrument. Divide into teams of three persons each. Each team selects one object to find as many sounds as possible with that object. (Consider textures, levels and registers)
    Suggested objects:
Typing paper (2 sheets), pair of cymbals (1 mallet), xylophone (2 mallets), triangle, tambourine, chair, glockenspiel, tissue paper (1 sheet), etc.
As soon as teams have completed their tasks, each team joins two other teams to develop

a trio composition. Each trio ensemble should have a common beat to unify their ensemble. Class evaluates performances according to rhythmic unity and contrasts in dynamics, sound textures and levels. Tape record the five most interesting trios.

7) Treasure hunts for sounds.

Each team of four to six persons should have a tape recorder, a recording secretary, and three sound scouts.

NOTE: Sounds may be classified in different ways according to their materials (wood, metal, etc.) or levels (such as high, low, etc.) or categories (such as machine, nature, weather, etc.) Taking the category of *places*, make a list, such as:

On the playground
Downtown (rush hour)
On the practice field
At a construction site
In the kitchen (rush hour)
At the zoo
Appliance store (demonstrating appliances)
In the dentist's chair
Garbage disposals
In the park (early morning)
School hall (between classes and during classes)
Swimming pool

Form the teams. Each team selects one category and makes plans. The idea is to find and listen to sounds in their category. Team members report on their findings and decide which place to do the taping. Plan carefully to save recording time and to select the best variety of sounds. Recording secretary writes names of the sounds as they are recorded. (Five minutes of sound tape are allowed.) Teams should analyze their results to see if they need to re-record. If there is time, further experimenting with their tapes might be done: trying different speeds or backwards.

When the different tapes are played for the class, each listener writes down the names of sounds they hear. Evaluate for the best tape and check with recording secretaries as to the actual sounds on each tape.

Did the taped sounds give different impressions from live sounds? Could a composition be made by combining your tape or parts of your tape with others? Two volunteers might like to try this for a future presentation.

8) Do some sounds have qualities or feelings or is it the associations that these sounds may have for us?

a) Name kitchen sounds that are pleasing to you. How about school sounds that are pleasing? Also happy Saturday sounds?

b) Listen to sounds for the feelings they give you, such as: fear, joy or anger.

c) What are sounds that spread and make you want to stretch or open?

d) What sounds shut or stop suddenly?

e) Are there sleepy sounds? Waking sounds?

f) Could you build a composition of sounds based on feelings and demonstrate each sound with movement reactions?

9) What kind of sounds command your immediate attention? (rhythmic, melodic, instrumental, alarm clock, etc.)

a) Is there rhythm in nature? Consider a season of the year. EXAMPLE:

> "There's rhythm I hear
>   In the beauty of Fall;
> In the call of the birds,
>   and the leaves as they fall;
> In the downpour of rain
>   'gainst the roof and the pane;
> In the moon as it rides
>   In and out of the clouds;
> In the game of the week,
>   And the stadium crowds.
> There's rhythm I hear
>   In the beauty of Fall."
>   —G.C.N.

b) Is there rhythm in the long steady swell of an ocean wave? Or, in fogs and stars and billowing sails? . . . In a typewriter, roto tiller, tractor, jet plane?

c) A poem by James Joyce, "The Noise of the Waters."* Could impressionistic sounds be added to this poem? Perhaps a clock ticking (use a two-tone woodblock) to introduce and continue throughout the poem interpreting the passing of time.

> "All day I hear the noise of waters making moan,"
>   (distant timpani roll and cymbal swell)
>
> "Sad as the sea-bird is, when going forth alone,"
>   (soprano recorder—blow on top section)
>
> "He hears the winds cry to the waters' monotone,"
>   (swish hand across hand drum)
>
> "The grey winds, the cold winds are blowing where I go."
>   (cymbal tremolo or sheet metal waved back and forth)
>
> "I hear the noise of many waters far below."
>   (alto met. and xylophones with sheet metal)
>
> "All day, all night, I hear them flowing to and fro."
>   (bass marimba glissando, gong, and woodblock fades out)

Could group movement be added? See chapter on movement, "How to move like one body."

This would be a multi-media and multi-dimensional interpretation using language, sounds, and movement.

* From *Collected Poems* by James Joyce, Copyright 1918 by B.W. Huebsch, Inc., 1946 by Nora Joyce. All rights reserved. Reprinted by Permission of The Viking Press, Inc.

B. Flexibility in Rhythm and Performance

Are the sounds in #8 even and unchanging, or do they change their speed and their patterns? What would be the difference if all these sounds were regular in their underlying beats? What effect does a steady unceasing drop of water have on the human being?

Raising Your F.Q. (Flexibility Quotient)
How flexible are *you*?

1) Experiment in walking together. Select four volunteers (two sets of partners). Decide which is A and B.

2) Partners will walk together side by side but B's are to match their steps to those of A's. B's will see how quickly they can adapt their walking and synchronize it, keeping with A's all the way. Twice around the room they'll go. A's are to walk naturally.

3) On next trip out of the room, we'll all try it in partners. Could you match your steps with an adult partner? A kindergarten partner?

4) Another experiment with four words:

"First come, first served."

As we speak and walk these words, we will clap on the *first* word of the phrase. Next time clap on the *second* word, third time clap on the *third* word, fourth time on the *fourth* word, and the fifth time on the *first* word again. (Each time we say the Proverb, we move the clap over one word.)

5) Experiment with flexibility in walking with *five* words:

"*First* come, *first* served, please."

This time clap on the "first" only, everytime; and dip your body slightly to add emphasis.

6) Alphabet games

a) Walking, one letter to a step. Clap on the first and third letters in a 2—3 meter pattern.

EXAMPLE: 1 2—1 2 3—1 2—1 2   3 etc.

Clap   A B C D E F G H I   J K L M N O P Q
       >   >   >   >   >   >   >

       R S T U V W X Y Z
       >   >   >   >

b) Try a 2—3—4 combination:

1 2—1 2 3—1 2 3 4—etc.

Clap   A B C D E F G H I J K L M N O P Q R S T U
       >   >   >   >   >   >   >   >

V W X Y Z.
      >

c) Two groups: One group starts two letters ahead of the other.

Group I: A B C D E F G H I J K L M N O etc.
Group II: A B C D E F G H I J K L M etc.

7) Check at home your flexibility quotient. How well do you adjust to changes in meal time if your mother is late? To furniture rearrangement? To changes in family plans? To unexpected chores and obligations? Being able to adapt to changes in environment, to new situations, to new demands, is important to one's well-being. Rigidity and inability to adapt are causing human breakdowns in our swiftly and constantly changing world.

Narrowness and rigidity do not prepare one for meeting the wide diversity of choices and the need to make decisions at every turn.

Flexibility begins with awareness-experiences in movement, (how freely do you move?); with the five senses, (children are capable of multi-sensory intake); with interaction that brings feelings and the intellect together, i.e. understanding other people's feelings and needs in relation to your own—this is confluent education—sensitivity.

Q. What is Tonal Sound? Listen and compare:
   1) A cymbal tapped; one tone on a glockenspiel.
   2) A woodblock sound; one tone on a xylophone.
   3) A metal sound in the room; one tone on a metallophone.
   4) Any sound found in the room (not a tonal instrument); a plucked string on a guitar, cello, or violin.

Q. What factors are common to all the above sounds?
A. They are all sounds, and all the sounds produced came from manufactured materials.
Q. Is there any factor common to the first sounds in each pair above?
A. These are sounds of *indefinite* pitch.
Q. Is there any common factor in the second sounds of each pair?
A. These are *tonal* sounds of *definite* pitch.
Q. What might be a specific difference between indefinite and definite sounds?
A. Indefinite sounds do not have an exact tone pitch frequency; they are irregular. Definite sounds have specific frequency, i.e., an exact number of vibrations per second.
Q. Can there be tonal sound of indefinite pitch?
A. Only if the two words, "pitch level" are used, meaning, general place, rather than an exact or specific pitch. The single word "pitch" in music means a specific frequency.

Now listen and compare different pitch registers within one texture of sound: play the longest tonebar of each:

Bass,	Alto,	and Soprano xylophones
(Low C,	Middle C	High C)

Close your eyes and listen. If you hear the lowest "C," point to the floor; middle C, put one hand at waist level, and for high C, raise one hand overhead.

Teacher then plays individual C's on various xylophones.

NOTE: Watch for students who do not seem to distinguish registers. Later, test these students again; ask for hearing checkups if needed.

C) Sensitivity Games (Supplement)

The following games may have little to do with teaching music as a subject. They are offered here to stir both teacher and trainee to greater awareness of human responses through specific focus of attention.

PREPARATION EXERCISES

1) To increase powers of observation.
On certain days over a period of time, the teacher or a student (different volunteers) places *one small* object (never before in the room) where it is visible, but not conspicuous, to all the class. The idea is to see or locate the new object but not to tell where or what it is. At the end of the day, how many have located it?

2) What sounds do you hear?
   a) with your ear close to the ground?
   b) lying on the floor with your eyes closed?
   c) when you run? when you skip?
   d) when you walk with one shoe off?
3) How does it feel?
   a) to write your name in the air with both hands?
   b) to paint a picture in the air, with an imaginary brush in each hand?
   c) to hold a polished stone in one hand and a piece of coarse sandpaper in the other?
   d) to receive angry words from your teacher?
   e) to catch a quick look of encouragement or praise from your teacher?

Sensitivity Exercises (To Experience Trust)

1) Blind Game

Partners A and B: B closes his eyes as if blind, as A leads him across the room to a pre-selected spot.

RULES: Do not bump any object. A guides B by holding one elbow only.
     Exchange Partners.

B faces A, puts right palm on his right palm, left palm on left palm. B walks backwards leading A to a new location.
     Exchange Partners.

A leads B up stairsteps with one point of body contact. B leads A downstairs.
     Exchange Partners.

2) Feed Your Partner Game

Each one feeds the other in the lunch room.

3) A Conversation

Partners Game, Back to Back

Importance of Eye-to-Eye Encounter in Conversation.

Partners sit on the floor back to back or on chairs that are back to back. A and B converse without being able to see each other. Select conversation subjects such as:

——What would you do today if there was no school?

——What might it be like on Mars?

——Your favorite hobby

——Your favorite baseball players

Out of this experience, students come to realize that trying to talk with someone whom you cannot see is frustrating. A back to back conversation is even more frustrating because the usual or expected reactions cannot be seen or sensed. It is somewhat like talking to a blank wall.

4) Discrimination*

    To develop awareness of differences in

shape, size, taste, touch, smell, texture, color, etc., in

    each orange, *each* apple, etc.

RESULTS: Awareness develops to the degree that there are no two of anything exactly alike, even grains of sand, or snow flakes.

Forming good judgments involves the gathering of a lot of knowledge and making fine discriminations and comparisions.

*Human Teaching for Human Learning by George I. Brown

5) Finding out about yourself. "What I like about you."
Circle game—One volunteer sits in center. Each one in turn speaks of something he *likes* about person in the center.

6) Earth Games

    a) "Dear Earth, I salute thee with my hands,

    Though rebels wound thee with their horses' hoofs,"

                                          (Shakespeare—*Richard II*.)

Using this quotation as a premise for a mime or speech game, partners plan their strategy. One is the rebel who damages the earth with his hands (pulls up flowers, scatters garbage, drives a car, pours waste into the rivers, starts a forest fire). The other mimes action of preserving and appreciating the earth, such as planting seeds, picking up litter, etc.

    b) How I feel about the earth, or what I like about the earth.

    c) What I would do for this town if I were Mayor.

    d) What we can do for the earth today—tomorrow.

CHAPTER 9

Hand Drums

A hand drum is a percussion instrument of many sounds and uses. Hand drums motivate participation and learning. Both a "virtuoso" and child's instrument, the hand drum is a delightful learning and teaching tool, which induces listening attention, aids development of rhythmic coordination, movement, interaction and sensitivity.

1) Explore the sound possibilities of the frosted head:

a) Brush the drum with your hand (weather sounds of wind, rain, surf). Try a brush (snare drum brushes) on the head.

b) Use the fingertips and finger nails in a fast, continuing rhythm.

c) Use finger pads—like mallet—releasing the resonance.

d) Try the large thumb muscle in a fast flick-like motion toward center of drum—a heavier sound than the finger pads but just as swift a release.

e) Try a mallet (not too hard, nor too soft a head)

f) Stop the drum resonance on the underside of the head with fingers of the hand that is holding the drum—a different sound texture.

2) Explore the rim of the drum for sounds.

3) Hold the drum between your knees and play with finger pads of both hands (as bongo drums).

NUMBER OF DRUMS

Although the ideal class situation is that in which there is a hand drum for every student and space to use it with movement, a great deal can be done with a lesser number of drums.

At least two different sizes of drums, such as 10" and 12" diameter, offer contrasting sound levels and weights. (Some students tire quickly with too heavy a drum)

Both plastic heads and skin heads are easily available.

Where the classroom teacher, music specialist, physical education and speech teachers should never be without a hand drum, there also should be drums available to the students.

Combined with speech, the drum clarifies and organizes the content, its duration, inflection and accents.

Combined with movement, the drum leads and focuses the movement as an extension of the body (arm) and it dispels embarrassment and tension.

Combined with movement and speech, the drum opens human interaction and eye-to-eye encounter—which is so needed by children of all ages.

Hand drum games

We begin with a one-drum game. There is much that can be done in personality, sensitivity, and coordination development *if* the policy of "everyone speaks" is established and maintained. Remember that the important thing is not the drum but the student and his maximum self-development!

Circle—One person inside the circle holds the drum like a bowl and travels clockwise for each person around the circle to tap a beat (circle moves counterclockwise). Everyone speaks the verse. On the last word "go," the circle stops and that person takes the drum, giving his place in circle to former "IT." As the verse begins again, circle directions are reversed.

"Speaking in rhyme and tapping in time . . . . ."

VERSE: "Rocket big, rocket white,
      Are you ready for your flight?
      Ten, nine, eight, seven,
      Six, Five, Four, Three, Two, One, Zero!
      FIRE! . . . . Out you go!"

(This is a favorite jump rope rhyme, contributed by Marguerite Drake, Los Angeles Schools)

Most any verse can be used. A good Christmas rhyme is "Christmas is coming, The geese are getting fat . . . . . etc."

An alternate version for inner hearing is to speak out loud *only* the first word and last word of the rhyme. Think the other words silently, keeping together by means of a common beat.

"Do Your Thing" Circle formation: One person in center with drum similar to the first exercise. This time on the last word "you," that person comes into center with drummer and performs rhythmic actions as the drummer accompanies the "dance." Drummer must try to have his rhythm accompany the dancer while circle people mark time with a clap/patsch pattern up to a pre-selected number such as 15. The dancer then takes the drum, and drummer takes his place in the circle and the verse begins again.

Suggested Rhyme:
"Rockets and pockets,
  Asteroids, too,
I like red peppers
  And weightless beef stew,
It's YOU!"

Leader plays a rhythmic pattern and while class echo-claps or speaks in ta's and ti's, leader hands over drum to next person. There should be no loss of beats.

Dictation: Leader plays a pattern—as   ⊓ | ⊓ | ;   class writes it . . . . . . after several patterns leader chooses volunteer to play what has been written.

"Pass the Tune Around" Circle Game. Class does an ostinato such as stamp, clap, patsch, clap, while one drummer improvises his own rhythm. After four or five times of ostinato pattern, player passes the drum to the next person and joins the class ostinato.

Two-drum games

1) Interaction (eye-to-eye) Circle Formation:

Person at 12 and 6 o'clock positions each have a drum. As they speak the rhyme, they walk toward each other to meet at the center. Each player plays the beat of the verse as he walks. After they meet they back up to their respective places *or* they circle around each other and go to partner's place in circle or they do-si-do and back into their own places. As the verse ends, everyone chants:

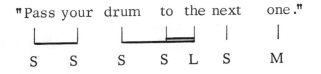

Each drummer hands drum to the one on his right and the verse begins again. Make sure that every drummer speaks the verse as he walks.

a) Verses: "Five, ten, fifteen, twenty
    Picnic lunch, we'll eat plenty.
    If I'm late,
    Don't wait—
    Five, ten, fifteen, twenty"

b)   "Seven, fourteen, twenty-eight
    Meet me at the garden gate,
    If you're late,
    I won't wait,
    Seven, fourteen, twenty-eight"

c)   "One, Nine, Seven, Two
    This is nineteen seventy-two,
    Work and play
    Every day
    One, Nine, Seven, Two"

d)   "One, nine, six, nine
    That was nineteen-sixty-nine:
    Moon walk by Astronauts
    One, nine, six, nine"

[1] Verses developed by different classes.

2) Drum talk[2]:

Two lines, facing: A leader at end of each line has a drum.

Leader I plays a rhythmic pattern as he moves forward toward other line.

Leader II replies with his own rhythmic pattern as he moves forward. Meanwhile, Leader I has backed into his line and handed over his drum to the one beside him. Without loss of beat, this player plays his message while Leader II moves back and hands over his drum.

[2] Drum Talk—can be a special message to the one across.
a. a person's name spelled in rhythm.
b. a line from a familiar song.
c. or a pre-decided rhythmic pattern or its variation.

3) Chain Game: two Teams (two lines) facing:

Leader I plays a pattern, then passes his drum to next team member.

Leader II repeats that pattern and adds one of his own, then passes the drum to his next team member. Team I player repeats the two patterns and adds his own. Team II player repeats the three patterns and adds his own.

If a player misses he is out and opposite team gets that turn. How long a chain? Which team lasts longest?

Pre-practice for this memory game is of great value and can be done without drum or teams by clapping the patterns.

4) Two Sets of Partners: open-end circle.

One pair of partners C and D stand inside the circle. The other pair of partners A and B stand outside the circle.

A and C each hold a drum so that the head faces B and D. B and D have one or two mallets each (rubber or cork tipped).

Then the beat is established, an ostinato is started on timpani or by class (stamp, clap, clap). Both A and C begin moving slowly backwards holding their drums so that their partners can play the drum, improvising a tune against the ostinato that goes on throughout.

The idea is that A and B team arrives inside the circle as C and D team arrives outside the circle at the spot where A and B had started. Moving gracefully, A and C can bend, stretch, or dip as they move backwards almost in slow motion. B and D players moving frontwards continue playing, listening to the ostinato and each other. The teams should never bump nor go between people in the circle. At the sound of a cymbal or other signal, upon destination, they hand their drums and mallets to next person and take their places at open ends of circle.

A new ostinato pattern is begun and the 2 new teams begin.

Class evaluates the performances on basis of interesting improvisations (sounds) and interesting movements (visual).

5) Forwards-backwards Spell Down:

Two teams—establish one unit or set that can be used, i.e. | ⊓ | | or any of

its possibilities. They are: ⊓ | | | , | | ⊓ | , | | | ⊓. Each leader has a drum.

Leader I plays one pattern, Leader II plays the pattern backwards.

If Leader II succeeds, he plays a new pattern and team member I answers, playing it backwards. If a player doesn't do it correctly backwards, opposite team volunteer may try it, and if succeeding, starts a new pattern.

Three-Drum games

a) Chain Game: three pattern sequence.

Three teams form a square of 3 sides, 4th side open. Each leader has a drum.

Team I leader plays a short pattern.

Team II leader echoes it and adds a pattern.

Team III leader echoes the two patterns and adds his own.

(Meanwhile, leaders pass drum to next one on team)

Team II member introduces a new pattern, passes drum. (II—III—I)

Team III member echoes and adds, passes drum.

Team I member echoes both and adds, passes drum.

Team III member introduces a new pattern, passes drum. (III—I—II)

Team I member echoes and adds, passes drum.

Team II member echoes both and adds, passes drum, etc.

Any error means player is out. Team with most players left, wins.

b) Korean Formation—3-sided human box:

Each side or person holds a drum so that it can be played by the soloist who stands at the open end of the box with two mallets.

The soloist improvises his own solo, playing on the different drums and at the same time dancing almost in place. He must try to make at least one or two complete turns during his solo. This means that silence will add to the beauty and excitement. A cymbal player indicates end of dance.

NOTE: After a few trials to get the idea, have different students select other percussion (claves, triangle, timpani, etc.) to accompany the soloist. The others provide a basic ostinato, changing it each time the dance ends. Example: Stamp—clap—clap—snap

As rhythmic and coordination skills improve, add drum boxes (soloists) and have the boxes each begin to move as one body, the soloists moving as they play.

This can develop into a stirring drum ballet with theme for development. Tonebar instruments can be added to the ensemble.

Many-drum games

Make a circle, using drums to join instead of hands so that the drum heads face towards the center. Two players inside circle with one or two mallets each. One timpani player who plays an ostinato (outside the circle) and one cymbal player.

To a 3-beat pattern, the circle members do a step left, bring right foot to left foot, wait.

The circle moves to the left as one player begins improvising on the drums and moving clockwise, opposite direction to that of the circle.

The second player begins, improvising against the first player. Both players must move around the circle while they play. They also need to hear the timpani in order to produce a good ensemble.

A cymbal crash indicates silence, and the players hand over mallets to others in circle who come into center. Timpani and cymbal player exchange parts and a new ostinato begins.

Extend the game by adding Indian calls echoed by circle as it moves. One person in the circle gives first call.

EXAMPLE: "Ay—yah—yah" (highest tone on the first syllable) which is echoed by the group as they move in step.

After three calls and echoes, the one to the left does three calls, etc. continuing around circle.

Other uses

A) In *Special Education,* the hand drum is an excellent aid to better speech and diction. For non-verbal children, the drum in his hands induces speech and reinforces the sounds, accents, and awareness of words. It is an excellent tool for motor coordination movement.

B) *Exploring space* with large movements.

Leading with the hand drum develops flow of movement and better phrasing.
"Drums play high,
Drums play low,
Drums play to the left,
And to the left we go."

C) *Spelling* difficult words on the drum, describing weather, etc. will make learning faster, easier, and more delightful.

Hand drums in the classroom can activate the apathetic child, draw out the child who is withdrawn, and bring laughter to the un-joyous lost ones. It brings a brand new feeling of success!

D) *Improvised Canon* Using Hand Drums

This is a gradual extension-overlap into an echo canon. Build gradually and consistently toward an overlapping phrase increasingly complex.
EXAMPLE: (The teacher might later use a contrasting instrument such as timpani or claves)

Teacher:

Class:

Teacher:

Class:

Teacher:

Class:

Teacher:

Class: etc.

CHAPTER 10

Hear Training

A "sensitive" in its recent connotation refers to one who has HSP, higher sensory perception.[1] Since tonal sound affects the known five senses, this aural sensitivity may BE FOUND TO REACH INTO HSP. All the more reason for early development!

"Sensitive," according to the American Heritage dictionary, means:
a) capable of perceiving with a sense or senses
b) responsive to external conditions or stimulation
c) susceptible to the attitudes, feelings or circumstances of others, and
d) the quality or condition of being sensitive.

Being responsive to external conditions or stimulation is essential to coping with and adjusting to the changes that take place daily. Perhaps this is the area where most adults fall short. We turn away from change rather than cope with it. If education is to be relevant to the nature and needs of children, then educators and parents must be responsive to change and flexibly able to cope with it. Consider how many "facts" of ten years ago have become misinformation today. Yet human learning and qualities of reasoning, evaluating, communicating love and creativity in all aspects are desperately needed in much higher degrees if we are to cope with our changing environment.

Awareness makes learning possible and it steps up sensitivity. Much research and experimentation with sensitivity training has been conducted in order to find answers to this human need, yet I believe that one of the most direct routes to developing increasing sensitivity is through the ear and specifically through tonal and rhythmic sound.

A statement to the effect that the sooner the range of sounds heard in the infant's environment are brought into tonal sounds of different registers and timbres, the more aware, alert and sensitive the infant becomes to his total environment.

This does not mean subjecting the infant to a heterogeneous or cacophonous mixture of tonal sounds nor high decibels of sound, which would be damaging. We should rather introduce sounds transparent in their mixtures such as in Haydn and Mozart, and sounds contrasting in textures and registers, gradually, with much repetition for points of reference and recognition.

---

[1] From the book, "Breakthrough To Creativity" by Karagulla, M.D.

As a result of working with different age levels, I find that this process is highly successful even if introduced many years after infancy. The purity of sound as well as the contrasts in textures and registers in the tonebar instruments which the children use and bring together in ensembles, increases their sensitivity in areas other than tonal sound. Although not measurable in percentages, there are noticeable behavioral changes which occur in many of the children. There are also an increased listening span, a receptivity as well as an awareness to color, motion, feelings, and language in their environment.

High and low—pitch discrimination

1) Direct experience-exploration with "high and low" begins with the body expression (See Contrasts in Space, verse page 11, Today With Music*) "How high is the ceiling? . . . How low is the floor?" game;

   a) Substitute a slide whistle for language to direct the movement response.

   b) Use a tonebar instrument—glockenspiel or xylophone, and up-end it (narrow end at the top). Play the lowest tone (longest tonebar) so the children can see it, then the highest tone. Indicate on the instrument their upward and downward motions according to sound.

   c) Aural discrimination: listening.

Show and play low "C," high "C," on the instrument. With low "C," hand is low, with high "C," hand is raised high.

Close eyes and listen—raise hands when the teacher plays high "C," and lower hands when teacher plays low "C."

Watch the class carefully to identify children who do not respond (hear the difference). Make sure they understand the directions and repeat the game. If certain ones do not hear, suggest further hearing tests for them.

2) Perhaps the high point in focused listening attention comes with echo playing sessions. Although it is based upon single performance, one at a time, the silence and concentration *are* electric. As one student is intent on performing the tonal pattern, everyone is hearing, analysing, seeing, and playing mentally the small melody they have just heard.

Rather than competing for highest number of correct playbacks, each one competes with *himself*, trying to reach a higher number of correct plays than he did at the previous session, which may have been a week or two before.

In order to understand the involvement experienced by children, examples and sequences of tone plays are given in this chapter. They are valid for both teacher training and for classroom use.

DEVELOPING PITCH AND RHYTHMIC DISCRIMINATION IN ECHO PLAYING

Echo clapping in numerous short periods (1 to 3 min.) should precede echo playing and continue in conjunction with ear training. *Specifics* in starting tone and tonal content focus the attention and accelerate progress.

* See also page 30, Today With Music: "Four Levels of Sound"

By starting with clearly stated 2-note patterns, rhythm and pitch can be combined in ear training. If a longer range of notes were used, where *only* the starting point "Do" were defined and stated (Example C diatonic scale), the rhythmic element should *not* enter into it and note lengths should all be equal.

The starting point especially with children, is *"So,"* the middle point. *So is "G"* the starting pitch. The first two-tone patterns deal with So—Me relationships, just as it is with their singing voices. Later on this same So—Me relationship will be recognized in Do—La, Fa—Ray, Ray—Tee; with transposition to other keys being only a matter of dealing with the same tonal relationships.

Pitfalls and meter changes

Meter changes in echo playing are usually a stumbling block unless the transition from a 4 to a 3 is carefully prepared in the leader's part. If many students miss at the meter change, they need more *Movement Experiences* in meter changes: Review page 96, combining with alphabet games and speech texts in chapter 8.

DIRECTIONS TO CLASS:

1) Remove F's and B tonebars.
2) There will be separate turns.
3) Each player continues until he makes a mistake. He keeps his own score of the number he reached before his mistake, so that at the next session he may continue or repeat as he wishes.
4) The starting tone is G. (T. plays G) Only two tones will be used—G and E. Notice E tonebar is longer than G tonebar. When a new tonebar is to be added it will be announced.
5) To help the player, there must be utmost listening silence. Any whispering or tonebar sounds and that person must forfeit his turn.
6) The player may ask to have the phrase repeated as long as he has not finished the pattern. Once he has finished the pattern, no more tries. If it is not right, next person's turn.

(2-tones So—Me (G—E)

T. plays on glock:

Use one review example as warm-up for each session

ANNOUNCE: ADDING "A" (3 TONES So—Me—La)

ANNOUNCE: ADDING "D" (So—Me—La—Re)

4 TONES

ANNOUNCE: ADDING "C" (L—S—M—R—D)

5 TONES

EXTENDING AWARENESS: MELODY BUILDING

Children are natural organizers, as evidenced in their play which contains:

logic ..... specifics ..... patterns ..... repetition and relationships ..... contrasts (change of rules) and extensions.

Beginning with a tone pattern familiar to everyone, the objects of the games are: 1) to listen and be ready with the answer. 2) to start the melody and extend the phrase, be ready with its repetitions. 3) to explore extensions of phrases, changes in meter, tone duration for change in a given song melody. 4) to explore possibilities. 5) to try mixing meters. 6) to try change of mode.

It will be noticed that these first experiences occur in the pentatonic scale with So—"G" for a number of reasons, namely; it makes for more natural and logical development because of its ease in manipulation, both playing and singing. It offers more flexibility and freedom for extending, altering, adding to and "combining with" explorations. It stimulates creativity!

We move from answering with single phrases to improvisation, then meter changes and mixed meters. When making changes in an existing song melody to see what the possibilities might be, we are led into an analysis and summary of what can be done in developing contrasts in musical composition.

Speedy melodic memorization is the natural outcome of early experiences with phrases and melodies as outlined here.

Play and answer phrase games

NOTE: In the following game, two students can be at each tonebar instrument. Watch for students who may have repeated difficulties in playback.

Game: (1)

T. "Everyone remove tonebars F's and B and locate G and E. Even though the different G and E tonebars may represent different pitch registers, you can all play together. This is an answer game. The answer every time is G—G—E. See if you can be ready and answer exactly together."

Play and answer game

GAME (1)

(a) Variation: solos

"Select 4 different registers high-to-low among the tonebar instruments. Decide which player will be 1st, 2nd, 3rd, and last to do the solo answers and we'll try the piece again."

"Are there any rests in the piece? Clap Them."

"Would an indefinite sound be appropriate to establish the rests?" (triangle or wood block)

"Play the piece again with the new color added?"

"Observe the interesting results of mixing instruments and sounds of definite pitch with those of indefinite pitch. Listen for such combinations in whatever music you may hear."

"Next time perhaps someone will be able to play my part or make up a T's part."

(Exchange Players—A New Group)

GAME (2)

"The answer this time is C, G, A, G, except that *you* play first and I must answer you each time. Those who aren't playing might sing D, S, L, S, with the instruments. Feel the beat together—4 times "1, 2, 3, 4 . . ."

(a) Extension: "Could you play 5 tones: C, G, A, G, and upper C. Again you'll play your phrase first. Feel a common beat—so count together."

"What happened? Why did we fall apart toward the end? Yes, I changed the phrasing to 3—i.e. an accent and meter change but you were still squared away into a framework of 4-beat sets. That's what happens to us in the face of sudden change."

"With flexibility and more readiness for change, do you wish to try it again? Establish our common beat—and here we go . . . . ." (Repeat the above)
GAME (3)

"This will be your piece. We'll all play a certain part together and four people will take turns improvising their answers. Here is our part:"

"Can you put the time duration of these longer tones into space? Play the phrase with one mallet only; express and feel space in the lift of your mallet following each note."

"For solo answers, use two mallets if you wish. Plan the order of solo answers before starting—1, 2, 3, 4 . . . . ."

Evaluate: "Did you like the solo answers? Were they different from the class part? Were they too long or too short? What made them different?—Rhythm, melody, length? Did the whole piece sound as if it belonged together? Did the phrases follow logically? Was the last answer a satisfying ending? How might there be improvements in the answers."[2] Repeat with four new soloists and a new group at the instruments.

GAME (4)

Every lasting and interesting composition contains repetition. Not too much, just enough—whether it is in stories, pictures, dances, sculptures, or poetry. There is repetition and a kind of unity in line and idea. There are surprises too, and contrasts, nuances (shades of repetition and change), and there is timing—a magic element which manages to put everything in at just the right time.

"Here is the tiniest kind of song (American Folk Song) that needs you to play the first

---

[2] More logic in unity of length; tonal melody contains these possibilities: repeated notes, step-wise notes and skips of notes, and silences. Also the ending of a melody usually comes to a rest tone.

measure. You'll ask the same question each time. This time, you will *sing* your part, and I will answer you."

"Could you hear repetition and contrast? Did it all go together? Was it complicated? Try it again, singing the words "Who's that," in place of Do—So. I'll answer you."

Text:
  Who's that—tapping at my window?
  Who's that—knocking at my door?

Repeat.
Next time answer
with class
names

Extensions:
Showing flexibility of song to changes, enrichments, etc.

1) Why not add some sounds that are indicated in the text? These could be the introduction and the ending to the song.

2) Where else could these sounds be used? (after every two measures)

3) Could other action words be used that add contrast and surprise? As:
  "Hiding in my closet?"   "Just behind the door?"
  "Running up behind me?"   "Counting up to four?"   etc.

4) How would it sound in 3-meter?

sing in 3

and in mixed meter

Change the mode by altering E to E♭. Reverse Do and So, to So and Do.

B. Such songs are indeed flexible, as they should be. This one has been subject to many changes, enrichments in meter, added sounds, rhythm, tempo and text.

Out of this small song and the changes and additions tried, come many ideas for bringing development contrasts into musical composition.

What did we try with this song?

1) Added new sound textures (claves/knocking). The melody was extended by inserting the new sounds between phrases.

2) Added changes in text in certain places.

3) Changed meter (which lengthened the song).

4) Mixed the meters: 3—4—3—4.

5) Changed it to minor mode by lowering one tone letter.

6) Altered one phrase by reversing the order of tones C and G to G and C.

7) We tried different instruments.

8) We *did not* try changing dynamics, to louder or softer.

9) We *did not* try it in canon.

10) We *did not* try opposing sounds that bring about friction when put together.

Project: Take a familiar song such as "Frère Jacques" and work in groups of 4 or 5. Have each group select 2 out of the 10 numbers above to do with this song. Each group presents their "altered piece." This could also be a Theme and Variations Concert!

CHAPTER 11

Classroom Instruments

- The introduction of tonal sound, especially in rhythmic and/or melodic structure, arrests all the responses at that given moment—unless the hearer has deliberately "turned off" or withdrawn from his environment.
- The presence of audible pitch, dynamics (degree of loudness) and texture of sound (quality or timbre) activates psychological organization.
- The earlier the child is in contact with and experiences tonal sound in different textures and registers (that relate to sounds in his environment), the more aware and sensitive he becomes to his total environment—because tonal sound affects all five senses.
- It is recognized that muscular and rhythmic media reinforcement can accelerate and organize learning process. Because tonal sound extends into all five senses it should be brought into the child's world as early as possible (long before he is confronted with an art form instrument, such as piano, violin or trumpet) in the form of easy to play tonal percussion instruments.

The following pages introduce and explain the Instruments in similar order as in the beginner's book of *Today with Music*. Related percussion and instruments for special effects are also included.

With older classes, intermediate and Junior High School a number of instruments can be introduced simultaneously for use in ensemble.

The purpose of this chapter and chapter 12 is manifold:
- to serve as a reference guide for the Instructor.
- to offer the reader a more thorough knowledge of performance techniques for each instrument.
- to explain the importance and uses of contrasting sound textures and registers in the classroom for greater individual development, including media for: focus of attention, alertness, mind stretching, memory retention and concentration, self discovery learning, self enhancement and well being, peripheral sensory intake, muscular coordination.

WHAT ARE CLASSROOM INSTRUMENTS?

Quality classroom instruments are tools of learning and a vital force for self development in skills (muscular coordination, listening, performance), aural acuity, language awareness, and total awareness and sensitivity.

They are specially designed instruments that are easily manipulated by the students. They include a variety of sound textures, such as wood, metal, drum; spreading, quick; sound registers such as low to high (father's voice to bird sounds).

Small percussion: (not tonal pitch but indefinite pitches) claves, hand drum, triangle, tambourine, maracas, finger and other cymbals.

Tonal pitch percussion with removable tonebars:

- Soprano, alto, bass xylophones
    with brown wooden or kelon tonebars.
- Alto and soprano metallophones
    with gray metal alloy bars.
- Alto and soprano glockenspiels
    with chrome-steel bars.
- Timpani drums—1 pair of "tuned" drums
    14" and 16" or 13" and 15" diameters.
- Guitar—in a different tuning from the classical or
    standard tuning.

Selecting classroom tonebar instruments

From a few instruments to many, there are principles and guidelines for selection. Select:

1) Quality. For children, instruments of fine textures and sound are of major importance. Defective toy instruments are damaging to the sensitivity and development.

2) Instruments with removable tonebars to allow for building different sequences and scales. Remove the other bars so that there is the least risk of failure or withdrawal, thus offering success in exploration, improvisation and ensemble participation.

3) Tonebar instruments that are tuned according to true-tone or just scale—*not* in the tempered scale of the piano. The singing voices of children are developing and growing muscles and the human ear is a very flexible organ, so flexible, in fact, that a sound heard three times is accepted as valid. Therefore, because a tempered scale is not true and perfect in its tone-to-tone relationship, it is *not* recommended for use with children's voices. Their pitch security and independences should be developed with or in relationship to the true tone scale.

4) Instruments of different registers and textures of sound rather than many of the same instrument. For maximum sensitivity development as well as for beauty in accompaniments to voices, the *prime factor* is having each register and texture represented before any doubling of instruments occurs. How much sensitivity to tonal sound could develop with 20 bell-tone instruments being struck simultaneously? Nor would much learning take place. The significance of these specially designed tonebar instruments for children lies not only in their true-tone tuning but in the beauty of their contrasting tonal textures in ensemble.

REASONS FOR CLASSROOM INSTRUMENTS

(A) Tonal sound arrests all human response

(1) stirring and awakening one's awareness and sensitivity through its purity and recognizable texture and register,

OR,

(2) blocking out awareness and sensitivity in a de-sensitizing bombardment of sound that is conglomerate, harsh, loud and possibly vertical in beat (not inflected),

OR,

(3) gradually dulling the alertness and awareness through a continuing sameness of harmonic formula and unchanging dynamics that lull one's senses. (Muzak; background music)

(B) Tonal sound affects all five senses

(1) awakening and increasing one's multi-sensory intake as the ensemble of contrasting textures builds in complexity,

OR,

(2) dulling the senses as in #2 & 3 above.

(C) Rhythm and melody are innate human forces at birth

This implies a basic need for expression and sophistication throughout life if the individual is to become a complete adult. This development should take a *linear* rather than vertical[1] approach, using rhythmic, phrased language (spoken & sung) *with* movement, *with* easy-to-play tonal and hand percussion instruments.

Without guided practice in doing two or more things simultaneously, such as singing and playing, moving and speaking, the student will not discover his greater potential for flexibility, nor find release from clumsiness.

Acknowledging that rhythmic sound is irresistible, the instruments offer an impelling, activating force (motivation) to succeed.

(D) Children by nature would sing before they speak, except for the fact that our culture thwarts this natural expression. Later, singing is an extension of speech, an expression in melody of joy and wellbeing for the child, a sharing that is linear in communication.

Although the infant's vocal muscles must grow and strengthen before he can sing, his song is there at birth—a three-tone chant, (So-Me-La) waiting to be uttered. This chant ("a tisket, a tasket. . .") is universal to childhood. Yet if it is not encouraged, exercised and developed, to sing may cause him embarrassment and insecurity later. Singing is a basic need of all children (into adulthood); in their language development for phrase flow, inflection and enjoyment of words. They should be playing their own accompaniments on the instruments and translating their poetry, interpreting it in sound textures. Again the instruments are the motivating, enhancing media for speech and song development.

(E) Tonal sound is a direct path to awareness

The earlier that tonal sound is brought into the child's awareness and recognition, the more aware and sensitive he becomes to his total environment. (See No. 1 of A)

Environmental sounds such as his mother's voice, sounds of wind, rain, songs of the birds, interpreted in tonal sound textures that are repeated for recognition, increase his awareness and alertness, his sensitivity, so that peripheral hearing, seeing, touching become natural to him. He is exploring peripherally and able to recognize familiar objects,

---

[1] See explanation of the vertical line and human development, Page 4.

beings and sounds. His reasoning faculties are growing with his organizing abilities. Encouragement of the mother in the form of stroking, singing, playing and enriched language expression (nursery rhymes) are vitally important for his well-being and sensory acuity.

(F) Rhythm is the organizing force in children's play

Rhythm has the same potential for their learning problems, if brought into the classroom in rhythmic speech with instruments, motor coordination and movement. Building ensembles with such media and reinforcing language expression with muscular coordination that is required in playing the instruments can open awareness to *form* in sound, language and movement. They can spell their words on the hand drum, rhythmically; sing their number facts; and write creatively, making phrases flow.

(G) Failure is not a deterrent factor in play, but a motivating force to try again

With this music making on (easy-to-play) instruments, failure or error only brings renewed effort to repeat the phrase correctly. Unlike the academic test, an error in performance is corrected on the spot, usually by the player himself, and the correct response is reinforced by its positive place in the total ensemble. . . . there is desire to contribute and to improve the total sound. . . . there is personal commitment to excellence.

(H) Music making, like play, should involve three of the senses simultaneously: ear, eye, touch

Bringing together the performance of a rhythmic pattern on the instruments with language text spoken or sung requires a listening attention to the ensemble for balance of parts; this exercises and stretches the mind far more than any one academic subject can possibly do. Thus, music making is at the core of human development.

(I) No masterwork in art form is too difficult for children to hear[2]

A masterwork reaches the individual at his own level and the impact may not be felt for a long time afterwards. Only the length of the composition and possibly its degree of dissonance should be considerations for the young child.

Recurring repetition of a few works are better and more rewarding than a continuing change of repertoire.

Dissecting a masterpiece before it has been experienced in its whole can be damaging to the listener and prevent his ability to receive the impact or enjoyment of the composer's work.

Live performance of a given piece is a hundredfold better than a recording. Recordings of the work should be played AFTER the live performance for real enrichment and enjoyment, memory retention and impact.

(J) Music has the components to effect total growth of the student

The inherent disciplines in music, its natural appeal, its intangible elements for "finding

[2] These conclusions are the direct results of Dr. Herbert Zipper's In-School Concerts for more than a decade, with follow-up studies. (Music Center of the North Shore, Winnetka, Illinois)

out about one's self," for releasing tensions and hostility, for stretching mind and imagination, place music at the core of the curriculum.

If a student is too tense to read and to work with abstract symbols, give him more music involvement with instruments that he can manipulate, and language he can enjoy.

School will hardly get better by isolating subjects and force-feeding with facts. It could come alive though with rhythm and melody, instruments and movement, opening learning receptivity and interests, awareness and sensitivity.

USES OF THE INSTRUMENTS

(A) to accompany students' singing, speaking and moving, in their ensembles. (Ostinato accompaniments; pentatonic scale)[3]

(B) to interpret verse, poetry, experience stories and art.

(C) to play instrumental ensembles in various musical forms: canon, rondo, theme and variations, song form, etc. and to develop notation skills.

(D) to improvise melodies and accompanying patterns, extending creativity skills.

(E) to explore and combine different sound textures in collages and sound scapes; to build new scales; to explore new colors of sound.

(F) to aid language development, phrasing, inflection, diction, rhythmic spelling and word sequences.

(G) to bring about aesthetic experience through tonal sound ensembles (group effort).

(H) to motivate self-expression through successful, rewarding experiences in rhythm and melody with irresistible materials. (the instruments)

(I) to develop muscular coordination with both large and small muscles.

(J) to increase awareness, sensitivity and peripheral sensory intake.

CLASSIFICATION OF INSTRUMENTS FOR CLASSROOM USE

(Instructional Materials)[4]

Textures: WOOD/METAL/MEMBRANE (Plastic)/STRING
Registers: LOW/MIDDLE/UPPER/HIGH

CARE OF CLASSROOM INSTRUMENTS

Musical instruments are like children: when they are treated with care and respect, their sound response can be beautiful and inspiring; yet when hit, banged or generally mistreated, the response will be equally bad. Nothing good can come out. Therefore quality in the selection of instruments should be followed by instruction in their care and treatment, plus established rules for their use.

It is well that students understand such policies from the beginning so that they can

---

[3] The ostinato and the pentatonic scale are natural and belong to children. See explanations on Pages 8, 51 and 69 of this Handbook. See Chart for *Pentatonic Scales* page 9.

[4] These instruments should be classified as *instructional materials* rather than school equipment because they are used in the learning process and development of students. This fact may be of importance in yearly budget considerations.

exercise judgment and responsibility for such instructional materials. Although these values and attitudes may be "intangibles," they are as much needed as basic skills in preparation for responsible adulthood.

SUGGESTIONS

As each tonebar instrument is assembled, check the tonebars for correct pitch and resonance. (Defective tonebars should be replaced by the manufacturer.) Make sure the support strips, nail hinges, etc. are intact. Irregularity can affect the resonance of the tonebars.

With *resonator tubes,* notice that the F & B tubes have pull-down keys on the Alto and Bass Xylophones for lengthening or shortening the tubes when F and B♭ tonebars are used. Call attention to this principle.

Warnings: Because these tubes are made of aluminum alloy, special care should be taken against denting or bending them, which would affect pitch and resonance.

Never allow the mallets to be placed inside the tubes. Place the mallets, when not in use, between tonebars, on top of the instrument or in a special receptacle.

TONE PRODUCTION PRINCIPLES

With mallet percussion the sound is *lifted* from the instrument with the mallet which taps it gently, quickly lifting it, allowing the sound to be heard. Suggest action imagery such as a bouncing ball, magic wand, or touching a hot stove. For best resonance, tap the tonebar at the approximate center   , over the resonator tube or center of the sound box.

Preparation for focus of wrist action with relaxed arms comes with *patschen* (leg-pat) exercises.

Further instructions and playing techniques are given with each instrument presented.

DIATONIC OR CHROMATIC INSTRUMENTS

Diatonic and chromatic defined

Diatonic tonebar instruments begin with tonebar *C* and extend through C Major scale (like the white keys of the piano) one octave and six tones.

NOTE: Each diatonic instrument is provided with F♯(2) and B♭(1) tonebars which make possible a number of scales besides C Major:
- 5 pentatonic (5-tone scales): See PENTATONIC SCALES Chart, pg. 9.
- 3 Major diatonic: C; F; G and their natural minors

- 1 Melodic minor: G
- all the modes: Ionian; Dorian; Phrygian, etc.
- whole tone sequences—partial scales
- new scales formulated by students

Chromatic tonebar instruments also begin with tonebar *C,* but extend chromatically (by half steps) like the piano keyboard—white and black keys. The tonebars representing the black keys are on a raised frame (sound box or resonator tubes).[5]

[5] With American made instruments the chromatic section can be added later at a nominal cost, and attached to the diatonic instrument.

Unless the instruments are to be used, continuing in the Middle School, it is advisable to begin with diatonic instruments. The cost is less, the instruments are more mobile and with the extra F♯ and B♭ tonebars there is ample material and tone textures for exploration and development of skills and understanding. Later, when students have gained enough basic skills in manipulation and explored musical forms with pentatonic scales, the chromatic frame can be added within the normal school budget.

It is wise and certainly less costly to start out with "diatonic" tonebar instruments. Additional tonebars F♯ and B♭, which are supplied with diatonic sets, make possible a number of scales and whole tone sequences for considerable development. The chromatic (like the black keys of the piano) can be attached to the diatonic sets when the classes are more advanced and ready.

Guitar:

Use a 6-string guitar, the three upper strings of plastic rather than steel. Re-tune it like a Gamba. Actual pitch—Bass Clef: low C_2—G_2—C_1—G_1— and 2 middle C's.[3] The two highest strings can be unison middle C. . . less breakage and with no major 3rd, only 5ths, 4ths and octaves, the sound is better for young voices. This also goes with major and minor. A *capo* raises the string pitches accordingly.

SELECTION OF CLASSROOM INSTRUMENTS

What comprises a set?

In addition to the hand percussion instruments (See *The Sound Wheel,* Page 125) there should be *one* of each tonebar instrument shown on the Instrument Wheel before doubling any instrument. Nine tonal instruments plus hand percussion can serve a class size of twenty students. For larger class sizes, add one each of the glockenspiels, alto and soprano xylophone; additional hand drums.

One set can serve an elementary school of three to five hundred students quite adequately.

The Wheel shows Alto Xylophone at the hub or center of the ensemble—because of its mellow pleasant sound that brings a sense of wellbeing (memory recall of the mother's voice), and its range that extends into the child's voice, sounds of nature and weather. Speech inflection, phrasing, melody and rhythm are expressed quite naturally with this instrument.

To build a set on a more limited budget, use the same principle: start with the Alto Xylophone as the center of the Sound Wheel; select each successive instrument according to contrast of texture and/or register until the set is complete.

Since behavioral changes are effected through working with *different* textures and registers, having twenty-five Glockenspiels in the classroom would not improve sensitivity nor develop aural acuity. It is the recognition of each quality and level of sound in the ensemble that is important, plus the beauty of the total sound. Herein lies the challenge of self development through involvement.

[3] C_2 and G_2 are two octaves below "middle C". C_1 and G_1 are one octave below "middle C," etc.

SUGGESTION TO INSTRUCTORS

When introducing the instruments, rather than "telling about" each instrument, encourage students to explore the instrument in a "Feel-Examine-Hold and Try" discovery learning process. Utilize their findings in the explanation and development of playing techniques that follow.

EDUCATIONAL CLASSROOM INSTRUMENTS

THE SOUND WHEEL

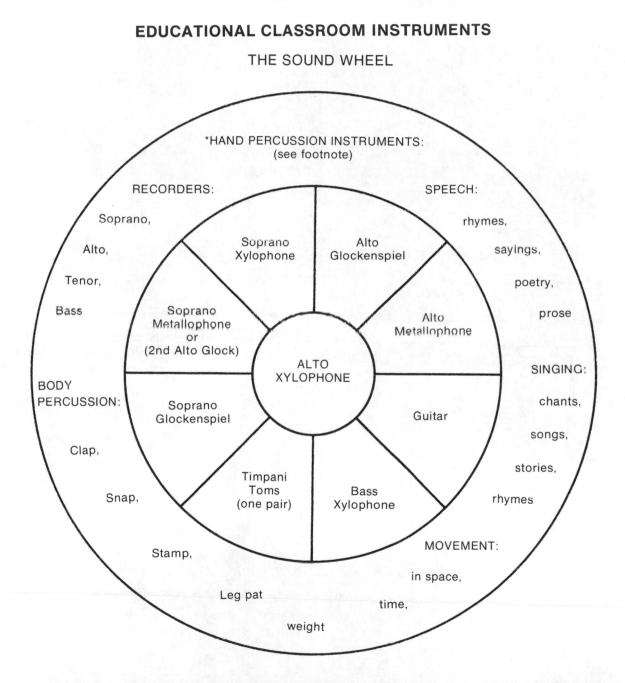

* Claves, Maracas, Wood blocks, Temple blocks, Hand drums, Tambourine, Triangle, Slide whistle, Cymbals, Gong, Whip, Rhythm sticks, Sand blocks, Castanets, etc.

CHAPTER 12

Hand Percussion, Tonal and Tonebar Instruments

STICKS

(A) CLAVES (Kláh-vā): a pair of short, round sticks made of polished rosewood which give a high resonant sound when played as follows: place one across the half-closed palm of hand with thumb extended for support and balance. Tap this stick gently with the other stick.

CLAVES

NOTE: Compare this resonant sound with the dull sound that comes with holding the Claves like ordinary sticks and striking them together.

USES:

for repeated sound patterns such as woodpecker, clock, knocking, footsteps, etc.

for keeping a beat, an off-beat or accenting a particular syllable or rhythmic motif

for echoing rhythms or word patterns ("See you tomorrow")

for spelling words (M-o-n-d-a-y)

for special effects in sound textures and composition

for Latin American and other ethnic rhythms

DESCRIPTION:

Claves come in different sizes, from four to seven or eight inches in length; (Latin percussion claves are even larger, made in a hard wood cylinder that is scooped out on the under side, and played with a shorter hard wood cylinder. Much stronger and more resonant in sound.) For young students, select small-size claves.

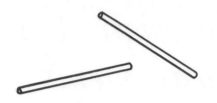

Rhythm Sticks

(B) RHYTHM STICKS

Made of polished hickory or painted/lacquered woods of lesser quality. Rhythm sticks are longer than claves, and thinner in diameter. Held in each hand, they are used as tools of sound, or direction in movement focus; in floor games for coordination and partner play patterns. They can also be used (1) as mallets for floor or table practice of instrument parts; (2) as rhythmic notation symbols that can be manipulated and ex-

tended into new patterns: | | ⌐ |

*See page 17 in TODAY WITH MUSIC.

(C) LUMMI STICKS

LUMMI STICKS

Pairs of wooden dowel sticks eight inches, ten inches or more in length and three-quarter inch to one inch in diameter. Their origin is New Zealand* where they are used in folk games and dances. Their popularity has spread over Asia and North America.

Usually a partner game, they can also be used in group formations of three or more; in circles or in parallel line formations.

TECHNIQUES:

For different sounds:

(1) tap sticks vertically ‖ ‖ on floor

* Made of native woods, highly painted designs, and with variety of sounds.

(2) touch sticks vertically ▯▯ (click)

(3) cross sticks ✕ (in front; overhead; at side, etc.) (click with partner's stick)

(4) silent actions
  (a) twirl R. stick; L. stick; both sticks
  (b) partners toss across R. sticks
      L. sticks; both sticks
  (c) pass sticks from hand to hand in circle or line
An interesting variation is a stand-up game using plastic tubes (golf club holders).

HAND DRUM

TEXTURE: Membrane/Plastic

DESCRIPTION:

Hand drums come in different sizes from less than 10 inches diameter to 24 inches; a shallow rim, one and three-fourths inches deep with single stretched membrane or plastic head. It should have key screws for adjusting the tension according to desired sound levels and/or weather changes. (Frosted plastic heads give a variety of sounds and the plastic is not affected by the humidity, heat or cold.

The hand drum is usually played with the hand although mallets, brushes or sand block can be used.

Avoid too large or too heavy a drum with younger students.

Avoid a cheaply constructed non-adjustable drum because of poor sound and high breakage rate.

USES:

In the hands of the student, it is a valuable learning tool; *combined* with speech it clarifies and organizes the content of words and phrases, the inflection, accents and duration as well; *combined* with movement it leads and focuses direction and follow-through in exploration of space, time and weight (it is an extension of the arm); *combined* with speech and movement the drum opens human interaction and eye-to-eye encounter so needed by children in today's environment.

In *Special Education* the hand drum can induce better speech and diction. For non-verbal children this muscular action and sound induces speech, reinforcing sounds, accents and awareness of words; also an excellent help in motor coordination and movement.

In summary, hand drums in the classroom can activate the apathetic and withdrawn child, and bring laughter to the unjoyous, lost ones. It brings a brand new feeling of success.

PROCEDURES:

(1) Explore the sounds on the frosted plastic or membrane head:

(a) Brush the drum with your hand (weather sounds of wind, rain, surf. . .) Use a snare drum brush on the drum for similar sounds.

(b) Use fingertips and fingernails in a fast rhythm.

(c) Use finger pads like a mallet, near the rim edge of head for a clear, resonant sound.

(d) Use the large thumb muscle in a circular flicking motion against center of head for a heavier, dark sound.

(e) Use a light weight mallet on the drum.

(f) Stop the resonance of drum on the underside of head, with the hand that is holding the drum.

(2) Explore the rim of the drum for sounds.

(3) Hold the drum between your knees and play with finger pads like bongo drums.

NUMBER OF DRUMS

Although in the ideal class situation there might be a drum for each student and space enough for movement, a great deal can be accomplished with a lesser number of drums, even from two drums. (See hand drums chapter in this book.)

Different sizes of drums, such as ten and twelve-inch diameter, offer contrast in sound levels and in weight of drum.

PLAYING TECHNIQUES

First technique:

Using the middle and ring fingers as the mallet, make a spring-action contact with the drum head that draws an instant resonance from the drum.

NOTE: Do not use finger tips. Use broad side of fingers through to middle joint. (Inside, not the back of hand.)

Strike the drum at the *rim* just south of the thumb that is holding the drum.

Practice this release-strike until the sound is forthright and clear, no longer resembling a wet cardboard sound.

Play the following notation in unison, then in canon with each player beginning one measure apart.

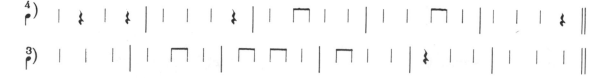

Say and play the proverb, "Early to bed. . . . ." Try other proverbs and join them together or play them in ensemble.

Make up word sequences such as names of cars, breakfast cereals, or names of classmates and play them on the hand drum.

Second technique:

This is done with the base muscle of the thumb, striking near the center of the drum head in a wrist-flick action that produces a heavier and darker sound than with the two middle fingers. Practice the thumb stroke for a resonant sound, then combine it with the first technique and play the notation below. Stems down indicate thumb muscle; stems up indicate finger lengths.

OTHER TECHNIQUES:

(1) Use finger tips in repeating action patterns, such as, thumb and middle finger alternating; first and second fingers, etc. With young children, to exercise small muscles in finger action, play alternating fingertips on clock beats to accompany speaking a rhyme and walking simultaneously. Example: Tick-tock, tick-tock. . . . . (drum) played with first, second, first, second fingers while the rhyme, "Hickory, dickory dock,. . . . ." is spoken. Try the middle and fourth fingers playing the drum beat to other spoken rhymes.

(2) Hold the drum between the knees and play with both hands like bongo drums or floor drums. Make up interesting rhythm patterns to accompany familiar songs and verses. Play these examples: (Stems down indicate left hand pads; stems up, right hand pads.)

Try other techniques on the knee-held drum: hand smash; slap; drag hand & slap; fingertips running across the head; cupping hand against the rim. . . . .

(3) Play the drum with a light felt or composition mallet while holding it with one hand. Explore space levels with this technique.

(4) One person holds the drum, eye level, while partner plays it with two mallets. The holder moves backwards, leading the player.

(5) Two persons seated, each holding one drum between knees. Player with two mallets, plays drums like timpani toms. (Drums of contrasting sound levels should be used for this technique. See pages 15 and 27 in Today With Music.)

OTHER DRUMS

Floor Drums	Bongos
Mexican Slit Drums	African Drums
Jazz Trap Set	Side Drum

And there are many other drums, Indian, African, etc.

TRIANGLE

TEXTURE: Metal

DESCRIPTION:

A nickel-plated tempered steel triangle played with a beater of same material. Triangles are made in different sizes from 3'' or 4'' per side to more than 10''. Because of the many sound possibilities with the triangle, several sizes and weights can be used in the classroom. Quality material makes a great difference in the sound.

The triangle should be held by a short loop of nylon cord, clipped to a music stand or table or held by one hand to allow it to ring freely.

USES:

Bell sounds in poetry and rhymes; in experience stories and to draw attention or contrast in speech, song and composition. For signals, clock striking (or alarm clock), movement directions etc. For the shy child, the triangle is often the first instrument he will try. It serves to encourage further exploration. Interesting compositions and contrasts can be developed with several triangles suspended for one player to use, combined with one or more contrasting sound textures.

TECHNIQUES:

To produce a good sound, strike the triangle on the closed side. To stop the ring, touch the triangle with fingers of the hand holding the instrument.

A roll (continuing sound) is made by placing the beater inside one of the closed corners and moving it rapidly back and forth. For a slower tremolo, circle the beater inside the triangle. Other techniques include a swish stroke on the outside, stroking one side, or using beaters of different materials.

TAMBOURINE

TEXTURE: Metal and membrane/plastic, with round wood frame

DESCRIPTION:

The tambourine looks like a hand drum with added jingles around the shell. Made in various sizes from approximately 7'' to 12 or 14'' diameter, it has a stretched head of membrane or plastic with or without adjustable screws. The professional tambourine is adjustable and usually has more pairs of jingles than the lighter weight child's instrument. Select accordingly.

USES & TECHNIQUES:

Like the hand drum, there are diverse ways of playing the tambourine and many different sounds to make.

(1) To accompany children's voices, use a light tapping on the rim, holding the tambourine like a bowl.

(2) Play in the same position but alternate the light tapping with finger pads or knuckles playing on the head of tambourine, or knocking the head against the knee with alternate knuckle sounds.

(3) Use finger pads on the head, like a hand drum. Use changing pads, thumb and finger, flat mash, finger tips, etc.

(4) For a roll, continuing sound, hold the tambourine away from the body and shake it rapidly with the wrist action. A professional roll or tremolo is made by wetting the thumb and in a pressing forward motion, circle the drum head close to the rim.

(5) Striking different parts of the body with tambourine head (elbow, knee, head, hip, etc.) will make different sounds.

Explore further for additional sounds.

MARACAS

TEXTURE: Wood shell with seeds or small pellets inside.

DESCRIPTION:

A pair of oval-shaped shells made of thin wood and containing seeds which produce a dry resonant rattle when shaken. Like the claves which once belonged chiefly to Latin American music, maracas now hold an established place in percussion ensembles and symphonic music as well as in vocal scores.

TECHNIQUES:

Hold the maracas, one in each hand: (1) use an up and downdown wrist action; (2) circular motion of hands; (3) extend the index fingers on the maracas shell to control the rhythmic sounds by tapping to start and to stop the sound; (4) tap one of maracas against palm of other hand; (5) random sounds are made by gently rolling or turning one of maracas in palm of hand; (6) holding both maracas in one hand and using circular or up and down, or side motions. Explore for other possibilities.

Similar sound effects as Maracas, but with metal textures are found in

RATTLES/JINGLE STICKS   SHAKERS   SLEIGH BELLS

Before playing the following notation on maracas or other shakers, clap the notation, making the accents pronounced.

WOODBLOCK

TEXTURE: Wood

DESCRIPTION:

Made of polished rosewood or selected hardwood in solid rectangle shape, with one or two hollowed slits just under the top side to give it added resonance. Its rosewood material makes it similar in sound to the claves. The pitch level is higher or lower according to the size of the block and where or how it is struck.

USES:

Similar in use and sound to the claves.

TECHNIQUES:

Hold it in palm of hand and tap with a wood mallet, a hard rubber mallet or one of yarn, depending on the desired sound.

(1) To produce a roll or very fast rhythm, place woodblock on a resonant table or suspend it with cord or wire threaded through the small holes at one end of block and play with two mallets.

(2) For contrasting sounds, insert fingers into side slits and tap on alternate sides of the block.

TWO-TONE WOODBLOCK

134   This is a tubular piece of rosewood or hardwood with corresponding slits on each

side of the narrower center strip where it is held by the player. Different sound levels are made from alternate halves of the cylinder.

CYMBALS

Metal bodied, circular percussion instruments that come in many sizes, weights and textures.

1) Smallest: FINGER CYMBALS (also called, Antique, Chinese or "cinelli") Their high sparkling sound adds color, charm and contrast to the ensemble.

Played by tapping the edge of one cymbal with the edge of the other cymbal. To project the sound waves over the room, shake the cymbals after contact or make figure 8's in the air with each cymbal.

Note: Rather than putting the thumb or forefinger inside the rubber loops, take firm hold of each loop with thumb and forefinger. This allows the cymbal to ring freely.

2) Larger: HAND CYMBALS (a pair of cymbals made in different sizes from 7" to 24" diameter and different weights from thin to heavy.) For good sound, select a pair of medium-thin cymbals 7" to 11 or 12" diameter, to be handled easily by young students. AVOID using a cheap, tinny set.

Hold the cymbals by grasping the leather thong or strap in each hand. (Do not put the hand into the thong.) Hold one cymbal higher. This cymbal strikes the lower cymbal in a fast circling-away-from motion.

For a repeating action, play cymbals more vertically.

For a shimmering sound, play one cymbal with the edge of the other cymbal.

3) Larger: SUSPENDED CYMBAL (a single cymbal that is suspended from a stand or held by a thong or strap, and played with a mallet or mallets.) Many different sounds are possible, depending on:

  (a) material of mallet heads (felt, rubber, yarn, wood, metal, brushes, hands or stick end of mallet).

  (b) how and where the cymbal is played:
- at edge of cymbal
- toward center
- underside of cymbal
- at center of cymbal

with one mallet or two mallets; for single sound or tremolo effect.

4) GONG (hand hammered from special tempered metals that are tuned and embossed for deeper and more resonant tone qualities.

Has spreading sound and is used for special effects such as, mood setting; peak climax; eerie, awesome effects.

From dead center to edge of gong are noticeable differences in resonance and depth, levels and textures. Played with a shorter and heavier cushioned mallet.

NOTE: Warming up the gong a few seconds with a light tremolo of the mallet against the surface, brings a longer and more spreading sound.

* For comparison of different sized Cymbals, See Today with Music, page 25.

AVOID using a cheaply made instrument. (It would be better to use an industrial soap can lid for sound than an inferior gong.)

RELATED HAND PERCUSSION INSTRUMENTS

(1) TEMPLE BLOCKS: Five blocks of lacquered hard wood in graded sizes for corresponding sound levels of clear resonant tones; *played* with rubber or wood tipped mallets over the lip of each block. *used* in fast rhythmic passages, to punctuate or call attention to changing accents in the rhythmic or melodic line, to vary sound textures; a delightful, teasing, provoking instrument.

(2) CASTANETS: (wood or plastic) Originally a virtuoso instrument played by Spanish dancers, the castanets are now widely used in musical scores of many styles. Mounted on a handle or block for easier playing, singly or in pairs, their rippling, rapid and piercing sounds indicate their use in ensembles to be sparingly added.

(3) SAND BLOCKS: A pair of rectangular blocks covered with sand paper on one side; *held* by the small knob on top of each block, they produce a swishing sound when rubbed together. *Used* for sound effects such as, trains, surf, wind, water, etc.

(4) WHIP: A spring stick of hinged strips of wood which produce a whip sound when slapped together. *Used* for special effects.

(5) RATCHET: made of hardwood with grooved nylon drum and metal sides; has a turning handle that can produce various speeds in raspy sounds for imitations and other effects.

(6) COWBELL: (hollow metal bell) *Played* with a hard rubber tipped mallet. For roll or tremolo sound, rattle the mallet inside the bell. *Used* for special effects, Latin American and percussion ensembles.

(7) SLIDE WHISTLE: (metal tube whistle with slide action handle) *Played* by blowing and moving the action handle back and forth. *Used* for special effects, weather, sirens, eerie, space or simulating of electronic sounds.

OTHER INSTRUMENTS FOR SPECIAL USES AND EFFECTS

WIND CHIMES (metal, stone, bamboo, wood or pottery)
CONDUIT PIPE (cut in different lengths for desired pitches)
WOBBLY BOARD (wood or galvanized metal; for wind, storm, etc.)
RUBBER HOSE (different lengths for different pitches)
GLASS GOBLETS, BOWLS (water added) for sustained sounds, rub top edges with moistened finger; tap or strike for pitched sounds.
BALLOONS (water added for special sounds; air fizzles, squeaks, etc.) KITCHEN UTENSILS, SHOP TOOLS, STRAWS, FOIL PLATES, COFFEE CANS, JUGS, COMPOSITION URNS, ROOM SOUNDS, TAPE RECORDERS, ETC.

HARMONICA & MELODICA, BARITONE UKELELE

TONAL AND TONEBAR PERCUSSION INSTRUMENTS

Classification according to texture, register, range and description

I. WOOD TEXTURE:
XYLOPHONES (Alto, Bass, Soprano)

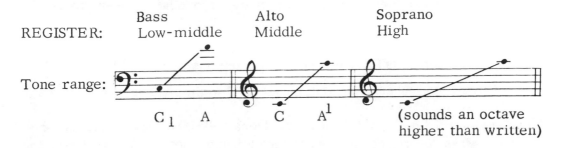

REGISTER: Bass / Low-middle Alto / Middle Soprano / High

Tone range: C_1 A C A^1 (sounds an octave higher than written)

DESCRIPTION:

Removable tonebars of rosewood or Kelon (fiber glass) set on a box resonator or a set of aluminum tube resonators. Sound quality is mellow, dry and even. Played with mallets of yarn, cork or composition fabric. For harder sound, wood tipped mallets are used.

ALTO XYLOPHONE (Diatonic)

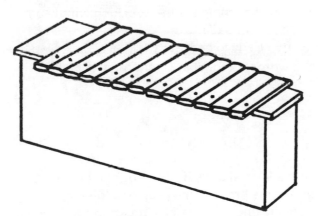

DESCRIPTION:

Removable rosewood or Kelon tonebars. Range: Middle C to A' with three added tonebars: F♯, A♯-B♭, F♯'. Quality of sound is mellow. Occupies center or hub of ensemble.

MALLETS:*

Strike the tonebar at middle of bar for best resonance.

(1) Take the mallet between thumb and first finger.

(2) Wrap the other fingers around the stick for secure hold, yet with a relaxed, free wrist.

(3) Turn hands over, face up, and check position of mallets.

(4) Now turn both hands over so that palms are down, elbows are out away from body and wrists can move up and down freely.

Playing the xylophone

(1) Explore the sound range from longest/lowest tonebar to the shortest/highest one. With each successive tone, try to improve the quality of sound, drawing out the sound by a spring action of the mallet.

(2) Remove tonebars F's and B from the xylophone.

(a) Using both mallets, place left mallet on C, right on G; play both tones *together*

four times: | | | | Take the beat for a walk, traveling over the instrument while speaking a familiar rhyme, such as "Pease Porridge Hot." Play the beats and speak the rhyme.

| | | | | | | | | | | | | | | | |

"Pease porridge hot, ⁊ |Pease porridge cold, ⁊ |Pease porridge in the pot, |

| | | |

Nine days old . ⁊. .|"

(b) Say other rhymes and accompany the speaking with two mallets playing the beats and traveling to new tones with each beat.

(3) Speak the proverb, "Early to bed, early to rise . . . . ." Clap the rhythm of the words, every syllable. Play the words on tonebar *C,* alternating mallets, left, right, left, right, etc.

♭ ♪ ♭ |.
"Ear - ly   to bed, . . . "

Notice that the left mallet is slightly north of right mallet in its position on the tonebar. With each repetition of the proverb, move up one tonebar: D . . . . . E . . . . . G . . . . . keep checking the sound quality and observe playing action for a wrist-spring. The faster the playing tempo, (the quicker the notes), the closer the mallets are to the instrument.

(4) Play other familiar verses, alternating mallets on the same tonebar. Suggestions: "An apple a day, keeps the doctor away." "Deedle, deedle dumpling, my son, John. . . . ." "The worst wheel of the cart makes the most noise." "Peter, Peter, Pumpkin eater. . . . ."

(5) Making a melody: (Tonebars F and B removed)

(a) Select one of the sayings and take the *words* for a ride—traveling with alternating mallets to different tonebars as the verse progresses. Repeat the verse, phrase by phrase, improving the melody until it can be shared with others.

* Repeat these four steps in mallet holding often to insure relaxation.

(b) Ask a partner to accompany the tune with a repeating beat on two drums, ‖ :‖

claves, or a stamp, clap pattern,

(6) Playing an ostinato (repeating pattern): This involves a repeating muscular action which can be carried out by the subconscious mind, as in street games, etc. Begin with the fifth, C and G or D and A. Play with both mallets at the same time in a phrased beat pattern to accompany speech rhymes. See ostinati patterns,*

(7) Playing with three or four mallets: hold two mallets in one hand using the same principle as one mallet. Index finger separates the two sticks. To widen the separation for larger intervals, stretch the hand beneath the mallet (last two fingers) or stretch the distance between the two mallets with thumb and index finger.

Suggestion: Practice with two mallets in one hand repeating same notes while single mallet in other hand travels in a melody.

EXAMPLES:

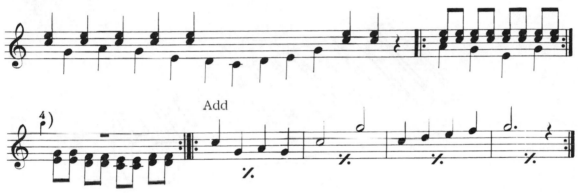

BASS XYLOPHONE (Diatonic) and SOPRANO XYLOPHONE (Diatonic)
(See page 137)

II. METAL TEXTURE:
(A) *METALLOPHONES* (Alto, Bass, Soprano Bells)

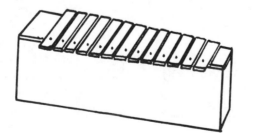

REGISTERS and tone ranges: same as above categories of xylophones
DESCRIPTION:
Removable tonebars of metal alloy set over box resonator; sound quality is a rich, spreading tone, bell-like. Played with mallets of yarn, felt or rubber.

* Page xiv, Teacher's Edition, *Today With Music* by G.C. Nash

ALTO METALLOPHONE: (Diatonic) removable tonebars of aluminum alloy that have a spreading, lasting quality of bell sound; played with mallets of yarn over rubber, felt composition or rubber heads. Tone range extends from Middle C to A'. (Extra F♯, B♭ bars)

OTHER METALLOPHONES: Soprano and bass.

USES:

In the ensemble the metallophone takes longer note values, slower parts such as half note borduns in fifths and fourths, echoing and/or changing borduns. Mallet techniques are similar to xylophone, to lift out the tone from the tonebar.

Greatly enhances the ensemble total sound; accompanies movement, especially in flow of continuous motion, slow motion; poetry interpretation and mood setting; expressive of time duration.

(B) *GLOCKENSPIELS:* ALTO AND SOPRANO (Diatonic)

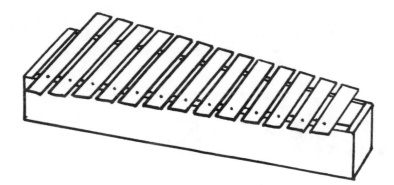

REGISTER: High

Tone range:

Alto	Soprano

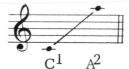

C¹ A²

(Sounds an octave higher than written)

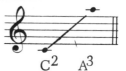

C² A³

(Sounds two octave higher than written)

DESCRIPTION:

Removable tonebars of tempered steel that are set over resonator boxes of wood. Sound quality is crystal and bell-like. Played with rubber or wood-tipped mallets that give a crystal "Tinker Bell" sound when used with spring-wrist action.

USES:

Ensemble parts range from simple ostinati to sparkling melodies and special "effects" such as glissando, tremolo, figurations, chimes, etc.

(C) *RESONATOR BELLS*
REGISTER: High
Tone range: varies with manufacturer.

DESCRIPTION:
　　Individual tone blocks set into a fitted case, chromatic, black and white steel keys. Sound quality is bell-like; played with rubber tipped mallets.

　　III. MEMBRANE/PLASTIC TEXTURE
　　 (A) TIMPANI TOMS (Tuned kettle drums)

REGISTER:　　Low
Tone range: one octave between two drums of diameters 14'' & 16'' or, two drums of diameters 13'' & 15''

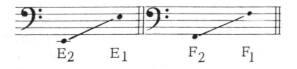

E_2　　E_1　　　F_2　　F_1

DESCRIPTION:
　　Tuned drums with open* bottoms and adjustable legs or tripod frames. Used in pairs to give an octave range and usually tuned to "Do & So", "So & La" or "Do & La or Re". The heads are of resonant plastic or stretched skin** with hand screws for tuning. Played with mallets of wool or felt heads; mallets are held between thumb and index finger with rest of hand folded around the stick, not rigid. Palms of hands are facing each other.

---

* Avoid a cylindrical, closed bottom drum in this size because the fundamental will not sound. The closed bottom produces the 5th partial, a major tenth above the fundamental which does not go well with children's voices.
** Weather changes, humidity affect the pitch with skin heads and require continual tuning.

(B) TUB DRUM (American made tunable bass drum, 12" by 20")

IV. STRING TEXTURE:

(A) GUITAR RETUNED in fifths as follows:

C_2 G_2 C_1 G_1 C C ; three upper strings of nylon
three lower strings of wound metal

Strummed, plucked or played with a dowel stick, tapping the strings.

Note: Having two top strings tuned to Middle C eliminates the Major third, *E*. With only fifths and fourths in the tuning, either major or minor mode can be used without changing the tuning or adding a fingering. This tuning also allows the singing to come through with purity, rather than against the heavy thirds and sixths that occur in autoharp strumming.

With change of key, use a capo or a dowel stick that extends across the strings to shorten them according to pitch desired. Older students can simply stretch the thumb across the six strings.

USES and TECHNIQUES:

To accompany singing of rhymes, chants; to interpret breeze, soft wind, dynamics, a sense of rest, wellbeing, poetry, experience stories; to add rhythmic patterns and contrast to a piece.

Different sound effects are produced with: (a) strumming or brushing the strings (b) plucking single strings in sequence or pattern (c) tapping strings with dowel stick or mallet stick (d) combining the above in a sequence.

(B) PIANO* Used mainly for special effects in low register and high register rather than as a harmonic accompanying instrument; middle register sometimes used for single ostinato, or for solo melody with tonebar accp'ts.

(C) Other Stringed instruments: 'cello, bass viol, dulcimer, quint fiddle, etc. go well with the tonebar instruments.

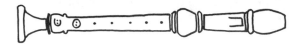

V. *RECORDERS* (Soprano, Alto, Tenor, Bass)

1) *SOPRANO RECORDER* (made of plastic or wood, flute-like in sound; tonal range C' to C^3;) PLAYED by blowing gently into the mouth-piece, covering the holes according to pitch sequences. A lifetime instrument. *Used* as an integral part of the ensemble, by both teacher and students in: taking melody lines, improvising interludes and rondo sections, to accompany dance movement and to play in ensemble with the instruments. An excellent readiness instrument preceding study of orchestral instrument. Can be introduced at third grade level if preceded by good rhythmic and singing experience with the instruments. Otherwise, wait until fourth, fifth or Middle School for class instruction of Recorders.

2) *ALTO RECORDER* (larger instrument in F, with holes spaced farther apart than Soprano Recorder) Mellow flute-like tones in lower register than Soprano; pleasing solo instrument as well as in Recorder Consort. Recommended for Fifth grade level and above.

3) *TENOR RECORDER in C; BASS RECORDER in F*

These complete the quartet of Recorders. A smaller Descant, Sopranino Recorder in F is sometimes used. It is like the Piccolo that is related to the Flute.

Questions about the instruments

The questions "If you could have only one instrument, which one would it be?" and "Which instrument is the most important?" led us to further observation and study.[1] The conclusions reached in 1964 have not changed, namely, that the focal center of the ensemble is the alto xylophone which has a mellowing influence on the voices in both speaking and singing. With this instrument in the ensemble, whether in melody or accompanying ostinato, the voices improved. Because the alto xylophone tone quality and register are similar to young voices, it helped the focus and quality of pitch.

As children's tone perception develops, their hearing depth also increases, i.e. they are able to hear *many* moving parts while they balance their own parts with the total sound *and* sing with their playing.

---

* The piano is tuned in the tempered scale rather than the justified, true-toned tuning of the instruments (tonebar), meaning that the piano tones are tempered approximately in tune in order to accommodate a keyboard length within the player's reach. For example, F♯ and G♭ have to be the same key on the piano, even though they are different in pitch. For this reason the piano is not recommended for young voices which need to acquire purity, accuracy and independence first. Also, children should be playing their own accompaniments on easy-to-play instruments. The piano is too difficult; it is a harmonic instrument and is usually played by one person—the teacher!

[1] Pilot project in Middlefork School, Northfield, Illinois, 1962-64 under direction of Dr. Herbert Zipper.

Their awareness of the different sounds, registers and timbres, and relationships (balance) to the total ensemble, heightens sensitivity with each session.

The general acceleration in skills and hearing acuity that takes place could not happen with an equal number of *one* instrument such as fifteen xylophones or fifteen glockenspiels. It is the *blending* of these contrasting tonal sounds that *opens* the child. "Opens what?" we were asked. The sound increases his awareness of beauty, desire, curiosity, exploration, effort, sensitivity and commitment, learning and achievement. He becomes flexible, creative and able to cope with change through his own working with sound and effecting change, manipulating melody, improvising and putting together. He becomes an analyst, a critic and a highly disciplined "doer".

With an alto xylophone as the center cog of the wheel, the plan is to add instruments of different timbres and registers, for the spokes of the wheel until we have three wood tonebar instruments; soprano, alto and bass xylophones; three metal tonebar instruments; soprano and alto glocks and alto metallophone (metal alloy); two tuned timpani toms and one guitar (string tone). At this point, a second soprano and second alto glockenspiel are added, then a second alto and soprano xylophone are added. We now have twelve tonal instruments. With the inclusion of fifteen hand drums and the usual assortment of small percussion[2], we have a more than adequate set of instruments for the average-sized elementary school.

CONCLUSIONS

In using these instruments as instructional materials with students of all ages and levels, the benefits are many, yet one large purpose is paramount from the beginning: to increase awareness and sensitivity of every student. This indicates that the *process* is more important than the *product*.

The significant results are not temporary ones but have to do with behavioral changes, coordination skills, extension of awareness in relation to one's environment, the feeling for language, for excellence and beauty, and a new freedom to learn.

There are two more intangible, unmeasurable objectives: that of experiencing commitment within a group effort to an end result that is greater than would be possible to attain by himself; developing courage to fail! This begins with an insatiable desire to play the instruments combined with the policy that "he who plays doth also sing (or speak)." Meeting this requirement in order to play the instruments brings repeated efforts; but as in play, failure is no deterrent, it is motivation to try again . . . and tomorrow is another day for trying. With each success comes a release . . . and the desire to try a more difficult part.

Practice games for mallet techniques*

Place left mallet slightly ahead of right mallet on tonebar *"C."* *Alternating* mallets L, R, L, etc., play the following words on a single tonebar. Move to the next tonebar with each repetition of the text. *Repeat* each line at least four times.

---

[2] Quality in the indefinite pitch small percussion instruments is also important—rather than toy rhythm band instruments found in so many schools.
* Use a C Pentatonic Scale with F and B tonebars removed for instrument games. Use Diatonic C Scale for 2. and 3.

I.

HAVE A HAP-PY DAY . . . .

COME A-WAY, COME A-WAY, COME A-WAY, ...

SEE YOU LAT-ER, AL-LI-GAT-OR, AF-TER WHILE, CROC-O-DILE. . . .

6/8) AN AP-PLE A DAY KEEPS THE DOC-TOR A-WAY. HOO-RAY, HOO-RAY . .

OLD KING COLE WAS A MER-RY OLD SOUL, AND A MER-RY OLD SOUL WAS HE . .

(Finish the verse)

II. (Going up the diatonic scale)

C	D	E	F	G	A	B

6/8) HIP-PE-TY, HOP-PE-TY, HIP-PE-TY, HOP-PE-TY, HIP-PE-TY, HOP-PE-TY "B"

(Down the scale)

C'	B	A	G	F	E	D	"C"

III.   (In a series of 8 eighth notes, accent 1 4 7 . with Left mallet;
Play the other numbers with Right mallet.)

C g g, D g g, E g

Add several Latin American melodic phrases to this accompaniment, such as:

Canon:

145

Mystery tunes for mallet practice

Stems up indicate Right mallet; stems down indicate Left mallet.

I. **4)** Remove tonebar B.

II. **4)** Put on tonebar B♭ (A♯) in place of B.

III. **4)** Remove tonebars C, F, & G. Put on tonebar F♯.

IV. **2)** All tonebars on except F♯ or F.

Use arm phrasing, lifting the mallets as if from syrup. Match tone quality between left and right mallets.

V. **4)** Remove tonebars E & B. All others on.

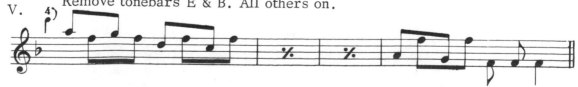

Rondo

Section *A*

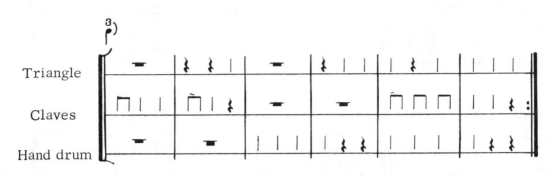

Section *B* (tambourine and timpani improvise)
Section *A* repeats
Section *C* (maracas and wood block improvise)
Section *A* repeats

Other ensembles

Suggestions: Play the text of different sayings or rhymes on the different hand percussion instruments—maracas, wood block, hand drum etc.   2) Divide the phrases among several instruments for interest; combine several textures in certain parts of the text.

Example:

"Early to bed . . . . ."

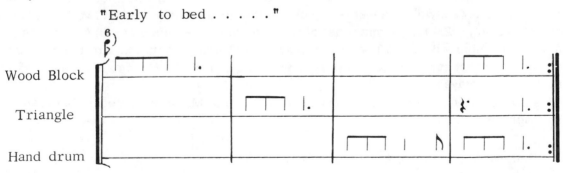

Add-a-pair percussion ensembles

The first pair of instruments begins and continues playing to the end. After four measures, another pair of instruments joins the group.......etc. The ensemble can be large or small, depending on the number of instruments used. Tonebar instruments such as xylophones/glockenspiels can improvise melodically against the percussion patterns.

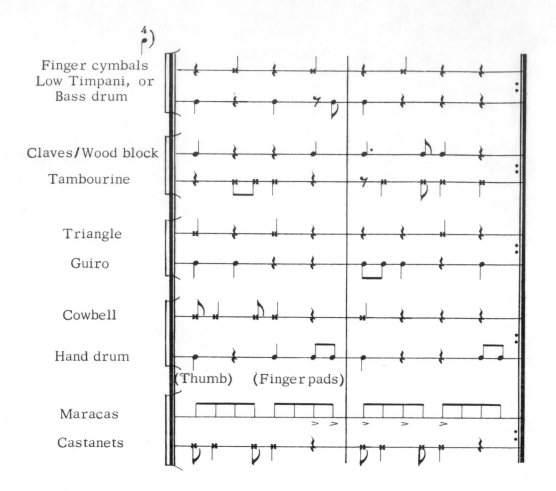

4)

Finger cymbals
Low Timpani, or
Bass drum

Claves/Wood block

Tambourine

Triangle

Guiro

Cowbell

Hand drum

(Thumb) (Finger pads)

Maracas

Castanets

Improvise with solo hand drum held between knees, or bongos; one cymbal, played with mallet can also be added. Use sparingly.

Suggestions: 1) Begin softly, add crescendo as ensemble grows. Reach climax then gradually softer as two instruments at a time withdraw until only the first two instruments are left playing.   2) Try different order of entrance for the instruments.   3) Add movement to the ensemble with hand percussion players with instruments that are mobile, move around the room as they play.   4) Make new patterns; design new combinations in teams of five or six players.

(Use arm phrasing, lifting the mallets as if from syrup. Match tone quality between left and right mallets.)

(Remove tonebars E & B. All others on.)

A bossa nova for xylophones and glockenspiels

SUGGESTIONS:

Alto and soprano xylophones can be combined in upper staff. One bass xylophone will suffice for the two parts in bass clef. The three parts on upper two staves can be interchanged between xylophones and bells, shared or alternately played. Maracas, claves and other hand percussion can be added to the ensemble.

149

CHAPTER 13

School Programs and Public Relations

Programs! For the PTA, for the school assembly, for almost any occasion, just ask the Music Department.

How can obviously detrimental aspects of this situation be turned into positive benefits to the students and to the Music Department that will reveal the impact of music for total growth and development?

Rather than produce spectaculars or elaborate operettas, consider programs as opportunities for extending learning-participation up to and including the time of performance.

SUGGESTIONS

I) Get information as to number and time schedules of programs for the year.

II) Make a plan for coverage of the various aspects of music making and learning that will go on during the year and include as many aspects as possible in the content of programs.

III) Divide programs among the various classes so that no class will be exploited. Try to have no more than two all-school programs per year.

IV) Make programs that will communicate to parents and administrators:

A) the role and importance of music in human development (music for total growth; mind stretching; concentration; esthetic experiences).

B) what John does in music class (content of music curriculum).

C) what music is doing for John's
1) self enhancement
2) listening-doing abilities
3) awareness & sensitivity
4) learning attitudes, participation, contributions, creativity, concentration, cooperation
5) personal enrichment
6) need to experience beauty and excellence
7) performance skills
8) musical literacy

V) Try to incorporate

—one or more learning sessions for parents (with or without children) which will involve parents in musicmaking ensembles such as their children experience.

—one or more demonstration sessions where parents observe students in music making as a springboard for children's own ideas.

—one or more occasions in which efforts of various age groups are brought together by a central theme.

GUIDELINES

1) SIMPLICITY of the basic theme will allow for creativity and development by the students.

2) At the beginning of the year, introduce BASICS that are essential to all musicmaking, movement, speech, etc., in material that can be adapted later for a program or used as a springboard for children's own ideas.

3) Work for FLEXIBILITY by having children explore possibilities in a given rhyme, song, proverb, etc. This prepares the way for extending and expanding a basic idea or theme.

VI) Establish certain principles of action as to time allotment for program preparation. How much learning time will be needed, etc. Here are some guide questions for consideration:

1) Should I be concerned with educating or training children? There is a wide difference.

2) How much learning time will have to be given over to rehearsal or mechanical drill?[1] Is any program worthy of more than two weeks of preparation time?

3) Of what value will this program be to their (students) total growth and self-enhancement?

4) How many child-hours of learning time will be lost forever because of this program? (Does the long-rehearsed operetta, the two-month old Christmas program have any rightful place in the elementary school?)

VII) EMERGENCIES! Sometimes it becomes necessary and important to present a performance almost immediately—to show a new curriculum or equipment—to enlist parental interest and support for this in-depth approach—or to activate children's participation and group effort.

To prevent exploitation or undue pressure on a class that is not "ready," select a group of children who are extroverts; or, ask the class that is the most mature socially and arrange with the classroom teacher for extra time during or after school.

Outline a cross section of material being covered in the regular curriculum and extend it into a learning-on-the-spot presentation, one that will highly involve the students in producing a fast paced music-in-action session, one that develops on the set.

[1] It is a well known fact that all learning ceases at the point when mechanical drill begins.

SAMPLE FORMAT FOR DEMONSTRATION PROGRAM

Music—a many splendored thing

1) It might begin with echo clapping that will be developed on the spot.

"Combine the two sets."

T.
Class

T.
Class

"Combine all three sets."

Class

2) T. "Who could write the three sets on the board?"

3) T. "Let's clap an ostinato pattern to accompany the rhythmic line."

4) "Clap this pattern and read the line on the board in ta's and ti's."

5) "Transfer the halfnote pattern to an instrument." (Timpani drums, claves or ?)

(Students make the decisions)

6) "Who would like to play the rhythmic line against the ostinato on a percussion instrument?" (Volunteer selects his instrument and the duet is performed.)

7) "Add a whole note pattern, perhaps on a cymbal using a mallet."

"Now, with two accompanying patterns, everyone clap the rhythmic line."

8) Set a melody to the rhythmic line based on three tones, S-M-L, each one in turn contributing his choice until line is completed.

9) Class sings their song with hand signals. Add the two ostinato patterns.

10) Add a halfnote bordun accompaniment to the song melody . . . build an ensemble of several patterns on the instruments. Volunteers who sing, play the instruments.

11) Present a song that has been prepared by the class with tonebar accompaniments. Use movement or rhythmic clap/stamp pattern with the song.

12) Add or develop an introduction, interlude and ending; an improvised new section on solo instrument; even original ostinati parts by the students.

13) Present a poem for interpretation on the instruments; in movement; or draw poetic phrases from class and interpret in sound, color and/or movement. (See chapter on Speech, in poetry, etc.)

14) Develop a speech ensemble from a proverb or saying.

15) Take several learning problems (spelling; antonyms; numbers) and resolve them through rhythmic expression. (See chapter on Music for Total Learning & Learning Aids.)

Central Themes for Programs

Seasonal:
> THE MAGIC OF SPRING (AUTUMN) (WINTER)
> THANKSGIVING FESTIVAL IN SONG
> CHRISTMAS IN THE COLONIES (Each class chooses one state)
> WINTER HOLIDAYS
> FEBRUARY—A MONTH TO BEHOLD
> PARADE OF THE MONTHS

Other:
> COME TO OUR CIRCUS IN MELODY TENT
> OUR DAY
> MUSIC IN ACTION
> EARTH DAY
> OUR TOWN (SCHOOL) (CLASS)
> MOON WALK
> AMERICANA

CHAPTER 14

Guidelines and First Lessons

Exploring the textures of sounds, getting the "feel," and learning about the care and treatment of the instruments—all this is not accomplished in three easy lessons, nor twenty, but in a day to day exposure and a continuing working-with experience.

Guideline 1.

KINDERGARTEN AND PRIMARY

The "younger" the children are, the more gradual the tonebar instruments are introduced. Meanwhile these children are using the small percussion instruments (claves, wood block, triangle, shakers, tambourines, etc.) together with their own clapping/stamp, etc. and large muscular movements which contribute to the focus and rhythmic control needed with tonebar instruments. (See pages 21 and 25 "Today With Music")

. . . . . It was Tuesday in late October. A rainy morning when the 6 and 7 year olds were describing Fall in movement games. Debbie was dancing raindrops with her fingers and elbows for the class when Robbie guessed and then said quickly, "But it wasn't right—raindrops make sounds." "What kind of sounds?" This started a new turn in pursuits. It was just the moment Miss Ferguson had wanted. While everyone was tapping on chairs and pencils, blackboard tray and a coffee can for rain sounds, she took from the closet a xylophone and 2 mallets.

"What's that, Miss Ferguson?" Pam and George followed her to the center of the room.

"Let's find out what it is," she said, setting it on the rug and lifting off three of the tonebars—F, B, and F'.

She handed a mallet to George. "Why not give it a try."

The mellow wood tones brought everyone running and crowding—

"The rain never sounded more beautiful than on that Tuesday morning inside our room," recalled Miss Ferguson. Everyone had a turn and we sang "Rain, rain, go away—It's raining—The old man is snoring—" We made up songs about the rain and danced to our xylophone with splashes and plops, drips and glissandos. The children even made up thunder sounds and lightning, wind, and a summer rainbow to go with their storm "opera!"

The next day this xylophone became a squirrel running up a tree, then a clock ticking, high ticks and low tocks. We did "Hickory, Dickory" and they made up their own tunes to go with the steady "tick-tock." What really surprised me was how their singing improved that day. There was Boyd who had never sung up on pitch. When his turn came (each one wanted a separate turn), he stepped right up, began his two clock sounds, and boom, his voice was right there and perfect!

They were still doing "Dickory Dock" the next week and looking around for some "mouse" sounds when the right moment came for the glockenspiel—with its crystal high tones. The rest of that morning we not only had mice going up and down the clock, but all kinds of birds singing. A robin, a bluebird, even a cardinal seemed relevant to that cold November day. We had conversations between a squirrel and a robin, and between raindrops and a mouse. Then—someone suggested putting the tick-tock of the clock together with the glockenspiel chimes—a brand new sound with the voices! What revelations of beauty!

Miss Ferguson's story could have gone on to the next discoveries: the soprano bells (alto glock) with its metallophone spreading sounds when soft mallets were used; the deep-toned timpani toms and how excited the children were as they spoke and played their names on those drums.

Guideline 2.

The "younger" the children, the less structured is the material. Most of the material and the direction of the learning is determined by the curiosity, interests and the experiences of the children at that particular time. Of course, the instructor has in mind large goals and more immediate goals, but what actually happens on a given day may be quite different from her outlined plans because the children take it by their route and according to their interests! Creative teaching requires a greater amount of thought and planning in order to allow and to guide learning possibilities.

INTERMEDIATE AND UPPER LEVELS

Guideline 3.

Introducing tonebar instruments at intermediate and upper levels requires a different approach; one that establishes certain policies on listening attention; on coordinating two to four behaviors such as playing and singing as well as hearing all parts; on pacing and balancing one's own performance to fit into the larger ensemble; on the care and treatment of the instruments.

Student committees to set up, check, and put away the instruments should be organized by the second session, with a change of membership periodically.

How to removed tonebars without damaging the framework, where to play the mallet for the best tone quality, the wide variety of tone with different mallets; which mallets go with which instruments; tuning the timpani; nesting the hand drums, etc. Such information should be given as needed and as the sessions continue.

Suggestions: (First lessons)

GAME: Place all mallets in a coffee can or receptacle, with mallet head-ends up.

Object: To find out and remember which mallets belong with which instrument.

As each instrument is introduced, the Instructor pulls the correct pair of mallets from receptacle and hands to player who demonstrates the instrument. Player then puts those mallets back into the can; next instrument is introduced . . . . .

Second team of players comes to the instruments. This time each player must choose from the can the corresponding mallets for his instrument in order to play.

CLASSROOM POLICY:

Instrument parts are to be practiced with fingertips rather than the mallets. (For the first few sessions mallets can be kept in the receptacle to help establish policy.) Explanation: by practicing or trying the individual parts with fingers on the tonebars which make very little sound yet give the needed contact with the tonebar, everyone can be practicing at the same time without distracting the other players. When the parts are ready, mallets are taken and the performance or ensemble is put together.

IDENTIFYING THE INSTRUMENTS AND THE SECTIONS
Suggestion: Use some kind of speech ensemble to facilitate learning of instrument categories and names. Example:*

"Xylophones have brown bars, brown bars, brown bars——" Alto . . . . . (plays) Soprano . . . . . (plays) Bass . . . . . (plays)
"Glockenspiels have steel (silver) bars——" Alto . . . . . (plays) Soprano . . . . . (plays)
"Metallophones have grey bars, grey bars, grey bars——" Alto . . . . . (plays) Soprano . . . . . (plays)

Suggestions: (First Lessons)

GAME: Disappearing Beat

Object: To focus listening and performance attention and increase memory span.

With mallets placed over *C* and *G,* play a given number of beats such as 8, (eight) traveling to new tones during the sequence. Follow with 7 (seven) beats played with mallets overhead, clicking each beat; play 6 (six) beats on the instruments; 5 (five) clicked overhead, etc. down to one beat.

Those not playing the instruments will walk the eight beats, followed by standing in place and clapping the seven beats. . . . . . alternating this plan down to one.

EXAMPLE OF Use of instruments with rhyme, verse, poetry

Recall a familiar rhyme of childhood such as, "Jack and Jill." Plan the sound interpretation, line by line, with one narrator speaking the verse. Share the result with another class. Try other verses, dividing into teams so that a number of verses can be presented. "Eency Weency Spider;" "Hickory, Dickory Dock". . . . .

Select a poem of Langston Hughes such as DREAM DUST and interpret in sound.

Design the story of The Three Bears in sound with different instruments taking the character parts. One narrator or several might be used effectively. Present the story to a Primary class.

Guideline 4.

SPECIAL EDUCATION

In Special Education the instruments are introduced one by one, with guidelines similar to those for Primary and with added emphasis on speech and motor coordination. (See Hand Drum uses in Special Education, Pg 105.) With the tonebar instruments come new vistas of learning achievements.

With these children *avoid* too much use of the ostinato patterned playing and/or marching in a 4-beat vertical meter. Use more 6/8 and 3/4 meter with as much phrase-flow and linear line as possible. Remove unneeded tonebars to assure good sound; encourage team playing in conversational style so that much listening to each other can take place, rather than attempting large ensembles.

Poetry, movement and color media, together with sound will develop and inspire creativity, imagination and value judgments more than structured, programmed learning. These children have much greater potential for achievement and self expression than has yet been realized. Tonal sound textures offer new paths for their individual growth.

Bibliography

I. Behavioral Sciences and Education

Adler, Alfred. *Understanding Human Nature.* New York: Fawcett World Library, 1968.

Allstrom, Elizabeth. *You Can Teach Creatively.* Nashville: Abingdon Press, 1970.

Ashton-Warner, Sylvia. *Teacher.* New York: Simon & Schuster, Inc., 1968.

Barsch, Ray H. *Achieving Perceptual and Motor Efficiency.* Vol. 1. Seattle: Special Child Publications, 1967.

Brandwein, Paul F. *The Permanent Agenda of Man: The Humanities.* New York: Harcourt, Brace, Jovanovich, Inc., 1972.

Brown, George I. *Human Teaching for Human Learning.* New York: Viking Press, Inc. 1972.

Cullum, Albert. *Push Back the Desks.* New York: Scholastic Book Services, 1972.

Dennison, George. *The Lives of Children.* New York: Random House, Inc., 1969.

Dreikurs, Rudolf, and Soltz, Vickie. *Children: The Challenge.* New York: Hawthorn Books, Inc., 1964.

Engelmann, Siegfried, and Engelmann, Therese. *Preventing Failures in Primary Grades.* New York: Simon & Schuster, Inc., 1969.

Erikson, Erik H. *Childhood and Society.* Rev. ed. New York: W. W. Norton & Co., 1964.

Fabun, Donald. *Dynamics of Change.* Englewood Cliffs, N.J.: Prentice-Hall, Inc., 1967.

——*Three Roads to Awareness.* Riverside, N.J.: Glencoe Press, 1970.

Fast, Julius. *Body Language.* Philadelphia: J. B. Lippincott Company, 1970.

Fromm, Erich. *The Revolution of Hope: Toward a Humanized Technology.* New York: Harper & Row Publishers, Inc., 1970.

Gardner, John W. *Excellence.* New York: Harper Colophon Books, 1961.

Gariepy, Richard R. *Your Child Is Dying to Learn.* Barre, Mass.: Barre Pub., 1968.

Gaston, E. Thayer. *Music in Therapy.* New York: The Macmillan Co., 1968.

Ginott, Haime. *Teacher and the Child.* New York: The Macmillan Co., 1972.

Ginsburg, Herbert and Opper, Silvia, eds. *Piaget's Theory of Intellectual Development: An Introduction,* Englewood Cliffs, N.J.: Prentice-Hall, Inc., 1969.

Harris, Thomas A. *I'm Okay, You're Okay: A Practical Guide To Transactional Analysis.* New York: Harper & Row, 1969.

Herndon, James. *How to Survive in Your Native Land.* New York: Simon & Schuster, Inc., 1971.

Karagulla, Shafica. *Breakthrough to Creativity: Higher Sense Perception.* Santa Monica, Calif.: DeVorss & Co., 1967.

Kohl, Herbert. *Thirty-Six Children.* New York: Signet-New American Library, 1968.

Kozol, Jonathan. *Death at an Early Age.* New York: Bantam Books, Inc., 1967.

Levin and Eisenberg. *Dilemma Series.* Toronto: Holt, Rinehart & Winston, Canada, 1971.

Lowenfeld, Viktor. *Creative and Mental Growth.* New York: The Macmillan Co., 1957.

Luce, Gay Gaer. *Biological Rhythms in Human and Animal Physiology.* New York: Dover Publications, Inc., 1971.

Luria, Alexander. *The Role of Speech in Regulation of Normal and Abnormal Behavior.* New York: Liveright Publishing Corp., 1961.

Luria, A. R. and La Yudovich, R. *Speech and the Development of Mental Processes in the Child.* London: Staples Press, 1968.

Maslow, A.H. *The Further Reaches for Human Nature.* New York: Viking Press, 1971.

——. ed. *New Knowledge in Human Values.* Chicago: Henry Regnery Co., 1970.

May, Rollo. *Man's Search for Himself.* New York: Signet, 1967.

Meade, Margaret. *Culture and Commitment.* Garden City, N.Y.: Natural History Press, 1970.

Mearns, Hughes. *Creative Power: The Education of Youth in the Creative Arts.* New York: Dover Publications, Inc., 1958.

Montessori, Maria. *The Child in the Family.* Chicago: Henry Regnery Co., 1970.

Moore and Moore. "When Should Your Child Go to School?" Harper's Magazine, 245:58-62, July 1972.

Murrow, Casey, and Murrow, Lisa. *The Children Come First: Inspired Work of English Primary Schools.* New York: Harper & Row Publishers, Inc., 1972.

Neitsche, Friedrich. *Also sprach Zarathustra.* Trans. Walter Kaufman. New York: Viking Press, Inc., 1966.

Nordoff, Paul, and Robbins, Clive. *Music Therapy in Special Education.* New York: John Day & Co., Inc., 1971.

Orage, Alfred R. *Psychological Exercises and Essays.* New York: Samuel Weiser, 1965.

Ostrander, Sheila, and Schroeder, Lynn. *Psychic Discoveries Behind the Iron Curtain.* Englewood Cliffs, N.J.: Prentice-Hall Inc., 1970.

Perls, Frederick S. *Gestalt Therapy Verbatim.* Lafayette, Ca.: Real People Press, 1969.

Postman, Neil, and Weingartner, Charles. *Teaching as a Subversive Activity.* New York: Delacorte Press, 1969.

Renfield, Richard. *If Teachers Were Free.* Washington, D. C.: Acropolis Books, 1969.

Rossman, Michael. *On Learning and Social Change.* New York: Random House, Inc., 1972.

Silbermann, Charles E. *Crisis in the Classroom: The Remaking in American Education.* New York: Random House, Inc., 1972.

Silverman, Robertson, Hawke, and Heintz. *Tomorrow Is Now.* New York: Holt, Rinehart, 1971.

Taylor, Harold, *The World as a Teacher.* Garden City, N.Y.: Doubleday & Company, Inc., 1970.

Toffler, Alvin. *Future Shock.* New York: Random House, Inc., 1970.

Van der Eyken, Willem. *The Pre-School Years.* Baltimore: Penguin Books, Inc., 1967.

Weiner, Norbert. *The Human Use of Human Beings: Cybernetics and Society.* New York: Avon Books, 1967.

II. Movement

Abramson, Robert M. *Rhythm Games Book 1.* New York: Music and Movement Press, 1973.

Barlin, Anne, and Barlin, Paul. *The Art of Learning Through Movement.* Los Angeles: Ritchie, Ward, Press, 1971. (Dance Mart Catalogue*)

Canner, Norma. *And a Time to Dance.* Boston: Beacon Press, 1968. (Dance Mart Catalogue*)

Driver, Ann. *Music and Movement.* Fairlawn, N.J.: Oxford University Press, 1936.

Dutoit, Claire-Lisa. *Music Movement Therapy.* Pyrford, Surrey, England: Dalcroze Society, 197?. (Dance Mart Catalogue*)

Findlay, Elsa. *Rhythm and Movement.* Evanston, Ill.: Summy Birchard Co., 1971. (Dance Mart Catalogue*)

Gell, Heather. *Music, Movement and the Young Child.* Sydney: Australasian Publishing Co., 1959. (Dance Mart Catalogue*)

Glass, Henry. *Exploring Movement.* L.I., N.Y.: Education Activities, 1966.

Gray, Vera and Percival, Rachel. *Music, Movement and Mime for Children.* London: Oxford University Press, 1962.

Jacques-Dalcroze, Emile. *Rhythm, Music and Education.* Rev. ed. London: Dalcroze Society, 1967. (Dance Mart Catalogue*)

Laban, Rudolf. *Mastery of Movement.* London: MacDonald & Evans, 1971. (Dance Mart Catalogue*)
————— *Modern Educational Dance.* London: MacDonald & Evans, 1943. (Dance Mart Catalogue*)

Mendoza, George. *Marcel Marceau Alphabet Book.* New York: Doubleday, 1970.

Mettler, Barbara. *Materials of Dance as a Creative Activity.* Mettler Studios, 3131 N. Cherry Ave., Tucson, Az. 85719.
————— .*Basic Movement Exercises.* Mettler Studios, 3131 N. Cherry Ave., Tucson, Az. 85719.

Michele, Arthur. *Orthotherapy.* New York: Dell Publishing Co., 1972.

Nash, Grace C. *Verses and Movement.* La Grange, Ill.: Kitching Educational, 1967.

Redfern, Betty. *Introducing Laban Art of Movement.* London: MacDonald & Evans, 1965. (Dance Mart Catalogue*)

Shawn, Ted. *Every Little Movement: The Principles of Francois Delsarte.* New York: Dance Horizons, Inc., 1968.

Snow, Aida Cannarsa. *Growing With Children Through Art.* New York: Reinhold Book Corp., 1968.

III. Language: Collections (Poems, Rhymes, Fables, Sayings)

A. NURSERY RHYMES

Baring-Gould, William S., and Baring-Gould, Cecil. *The Annotated Mother Goose.* New York: Clarkson N. Potter, Inc., 1970.

DeAngeli, Marguerite. *Book of Nursery and Mother Goose Rhymes.* Garden City, N.Y.: Doubleday & Company, 1954.

Grosset. *The Grosset Treasury of Nursery Rhymes and Stories.* New York: Grosset & Dunlap, Inc., 1968.

Mother Goose Book, The. Mount Vernon, New York: Peter Pauper Press, 1946.

Mother Goose's Melodies: Facsimile of the Original Munroe & Francis. New York: Dover Publications, Inc., 1970.

Newell, William W. *Games and Songs of American Children.* Second ed. New York: Dover Publications, Inc., 1903.

Opie, Iona and Opie, Peter. *The Lore & Language of Schoolchildren.* Fairlawn, N.J.: Oxford University Press, 1959.

Rossetti, Christine G. *Sing Song Nursery Rhyme Book.* New York: Dover Publications, Inc., 1969.

Withers, Carl. *Counting Out Rhymes.* New York: Dover Publications, Inc., 1970.

B. POEMS

Arbuthnot, May H. *The Arbuthnot Anthology of Children's Literature.* Rev. ed. New York: Lothrop, Lee & Shephard Co., 1971.

De Regeniers, Beatrice S. et al. *Poems Children Will Sit Still For.* New York: Citation Press, 1969.

Ferris, Helen, ed. *Favorite Poems, Old and New.* Garden City, N.Y.: Doubleday & Company, Inc., 1957.

Japanese Haiku Series. Mount Vernon, N.Y.: Peter Pauper Press, 1960.

*The Dance Mart: Box 48, Homecrest Station, Brooklyn, New York 11229.

Koch, Kenneth. *Wishes, Lies and Dreams*. New York: Vintage Trade Books, 1970.

Larrick, Nancy. *Poetry for Holidays*. Champaign, Ill.: Garrand Publishing Co., 1966.

Lawrence, Marjory. *A Beginning Book of Poems*. Reading, Ma.: Addison-Wesley, 1967.

————. *An Invitation to Poetry*. Boston: Addison-Wesley.

Lewis, Richard, ed. *Miracles: Poems by Children of the English-Speaking World*. New York: Simon & Schuster, Inc., 1966.

————. *Out of the Earth I Sing*. New York: Norton & Company, Inc., 1968.

Peck, Richard. *Sounds and Silences: Poetry for Now*. New York: Delacorte Press, 1970.

Tashjian, Virginia. *Juba This and Juba That*. Boston: Little Brown & Co., 1969.

Withers, Carl A. *Rocket in My Pocket: Rhymes and Chants of Young Americans*. New York: Holt, Rinehart & Winston, Inc., 1948.

C. FABLES

Bierce, Ambrose. *Fantastic Fables*. New York: Dover Publications Inc., 1970.

McGovern, Ann. *Aesop's Fables*. New York: Scholastic Book Services, 1972.

D. SAYINGS

Bacheldor, Louise. *Little Things: Sayings*. Mount Vernon, N.Y.: Peter Pauper Press, 1969.

Kredel, Fritz. *Proverbs to Live By*. Kansas City, Mo.: Hallmark Co., 1968.

Nash, Grace C. *Rhythmic Speech Ensembles*. Scottsdale, Az.: Nash Publications, 1966.

Rosenzweig, Paul. *The Book of Proverbs*. New York: Philosophical Library Publishers, 1965.

E. MYTHS

Bullfinch. *Famous Greek Myths and Legends*. New York: Pyramid Books, 1967.

IV. Language-Poetry

Ciardi, John. *I Met a Man*. San Jose: H.M. Gousha Co., 1961.

————. *You Read to Me: I'll Read to You*. Philadelphia: J.B. Lippincott Company, 1961.

Emrich, Duncan. *Folklore on the American Land*. Boston: Little Brown & Co., 1972.

Frostic, Gwen. *A Walk With Me*. Benzonia, Mich.: Presscraft Papers, 1958.

————. *To Those Who See*. Benzonia, Mich.: Presscraft Papers, 1965.

————. *These Things Are Ours*. Benzonia, Mich.: Presscraft Papers, 1960.

Gilbert, Edna. *A Way With Words*. (Creative Writing) Reading, England: Educational Explorers, Ltd., 1968.

Hughes, Langston. *Ask Your Mama: 12 Moods for Jazz*. New York: Alfred A. Knopf, Inc., 1969.

————. *The Dream Keeper*. 1932.

————. *Selected Poems*. 1959.

Leedy, Jack L. *Poetry Therapy: The Use of Poetry in the Treatment of Emotional Disorders*. Philadelphia: J. B. Lippincott Company, 1969.

Martin, Bill Jr. *Sounds of Language* Series. New York: Holt, Rinehart and Winston, Inc., 1972.

McCord, David. *Every Time I Climb a Tree*. Boston: Little Brown & Co., 1967.

————. *Far and Few*. Boston: Little Brown & Co., 1952.

Merriam, Eve. *Catch a Little Rhyme*. New York: Atheneum Publishers, 1966.

Milne, A. A. *Now We Are Six*. Rev. ed. New York: E.P. Dutton & Co., Inc., 1961.

————. *When We Were Very Young*. New York: E.P. Dutton & Co., Inc., 1961.

Nash, Grace C. *Verses and Movement*. Scottsdale, Az.: Nash Publications, 1967.

O'Neill, Mary. *Words, Words, Words*. Garden City, N.Y.: Doubleday & Company, Inc., 1966.

————. *Take a Number*. Garden City, N.Y.: Doubleday & Company, Inc., 1968.

————. *Hailstones and Halibut Bones*. Garden City, N.Y.: Doubleday & Company, Inc., 1961.

Pellowski, Anne. *Have You Seen a Comet?* (Children's Art and Writing from Around the World) New York: The John Day Co., 1971.

V. Music

Bacon, Denise. *Let's Sing Together, Kodaly Concept, Early Years*. Wellesley, Mass.: Kodaly Musical Training Institute Inc., 1972.

Carley, Isabel. *Recorder Improvisation and Technique*. Indianapolis: Carley Publications, 1970.

Collier, Corlu. *Recorder Song Method*. Berkeley, Calif.: C.E.R.C. Publications, 1971.

Darazs and Jay. *Sight and Sound*. New York: Boosey & Hawkes, 1965.

Dennis, Brian. *Experimental Music in Schools: Towards a New World of Sound*. Fairlawn, N.J.: Oxford University Press, 1970.

Ehret, Walter, and Evans, George. *International Book of Christmas Carols*. Englewood Cliffs, N.J.: Prentice-Hall, Inc., 1963.

Grissom, Mary Allen. *The Negro Sings a New Heaven*. New York: Dover Publications, Inc., 1969.

Grossman, Norman. *Book of Today's Drumming; Universal Rhythm*. New York: Amsco, 1971.

Jones, Bessie and Hawes, Bess L. *Step It Down: Games, Plays and Stories from the Afro-American Heritage*. New York: Harper & Row Publishers, Inc., 1972.

Kodaly, Zoltan. *The Kodaly Choral Method*. Progressive Series. New York: Boosey & Hawkes, 1952-1963.

Landeck, Beatrice. *Folk Songs of the Americas*. New York: Frank Music Corp., 1961 & 1964.

Landeck and Crook. *Wake Up and Sing!* New York: Marks/Morrow Pub., 1969.

Langstaff, Nancy and Langstaff, John, eds. *Jim Along Josie*. New York: Harcourt, Brace & Jovanovich, 1969.

Linde, Hans-Martin. *The Little Exercise* (Recorder) New York: Associated Music Pub., 1960.

Lomax, Alan. *The Folk Songs of North America*. Garden City, N.Y.: Doubleday & Company, Inc., 1960.

McNair and Nash. *Chorister's Manual*. La Grange, Ill.: Kitching Educational, 1968.

Nash, Grace C. *Music With Children: Series I. Series II. Recorder for Beginners*. 1965. *Rhythmic Speech Ensembles*. Series III. 1966. *Verses and Movement*. 1967. *Teacher's Manual*. 1970. *Chamber Music for Tonebar Instruments and Recorder*. 1971. *Recorder Ensembles*. 1973. *Music in the Middle School*, Series IV. 1973. Scottsdale, Az.: Nash Publications.

———. *Music With Children Films 1-4,* 16mm color/sound. Scottsdale, Az.: Swartwout Film Productions, 1968.

———. *Today With Music. Today With Music, Teacher's Annotated Edition.* Port Washington, N.Y.: Alfred Publishing Co., 1973.

Nichols, Elizabeth. *Orff Instrument Source Book,* volumes I & II. Morristown, N.J.: Silver Burdett Co., 1970.

Orff, Carl - Keetman, Gunild. *Orff-Schulwerk, Music For Children.* Series; English Adaptation by Doreen Hall and Arnold Walter. Munich: B. Schott's Sohne, 1955. (U.S.A.: New York, Belwin, Inc.)

Orff-Institute Year Book, 1962. Munich: B. Schott's Sohne, 1963.

Oxford Book of Carols. Ed. by Percy Dermer et al. Fairlawn, N.J.: Oxford University Press, 1964.

Poston, Elizabeth, ed. *The Second Penguin Book of Christmas Carols.* Baltimore: Penguin Books, Inc., 1971.

Richards, Mary Helen. Series of Publications from *The Richards Institute of Music Education and Research.* Portola Valley, Ca., 1970-.

Seeger, Ruth C. *American Folk Songs for Children.* Garden City, N.Y.: Doubleday & Company, Inc., 1950.

———. *American Folk Songs for Christmas.* 1953.

Szabo, Helga. *The Kodaly Concept of Music Education; Textbook & Records.* New York: Boosey & Hawkes, 1969.

Welsh, J. Robert. *Making Music at the Keyboard,* Bk. One; Bk One Supplement. Chicago: Ludwig Industries, 1969.

Wheeler, Lawrence, and Raebeck, Lois. *Orff and Kodaly Adapted for the Elementary School.* Dubuque, Iowa: William C. Brown & Co., 1972.

Wuytak, Joseph. *Musical Creativity, Bolero, Colores, Polyvitamins, Musica Viva.* Paris: A. Leduc, 1970 and 1972. U.S.A. St. Louis: Magna Music, Baton Co.

VI. Books About Music

Buttree, Julia M. *Rhythm of the Red Man.* New York: Barnes Publishers (out of print), 1930.

Coker, Jerry. *Improvising Jazz.* Englewood Cliffs, N.J.: Prentice-Hall Inc., 1964.

Coker, Casale, Campbell, and Greene. *Patterns for Jazz.* Lebanon, Ind.: Studio Publications, 1970.

Einert and Stockhausen. *Die Riehe: 1. Electronic Music.* Bryn Mawr, Pa.: Presser Company, 1958.

Fux, Johann J. *Steps to Parnassus; Counterpoint Study.* Ed. and trans. Alfred Mann, New York: W.W. Norton & Co., 1965.

Gaston, E. Thayer. *Music in Therapy.* New York: The Macmillan Co., 1968.

Hughes, Langston. *First Book of Rhythms.* New York: Franklin Watts, Inc., 1954.

Landis and Carder. *Eclectic Curriculum in American Music Education; Contributions of Dalcroze, Kodaly and Orff.* Washington, D.C.: Music Educators National Conference, 1972.

Malm, William P. *Music Cultures of the Pacific, the Near East and Asia.* Englewood Cliffs, N.J.: Prentice-Hall, Inc., 1966.

Marsh, Mary V. *Explore and Discover Music.* New York: The Macmillan Co., 1970.

McCloskey, David Blair. *Your Voice at Its Best.* Plymouth, Mass.: Memorial Press.

Meyer, Leonard B. *Emotion and Meaning in Music.* Chicago: University of Chicago Press, 1956.

Orff-Institute Year Book, 1962. Munich: B. Schott's Sohne, 1963.

Pillsbury Foundation Studies Report: Music of Young Children. (P.O. Drawer H-H Santa Barbara, Ca. 93102) This is the address for obtaining this Report)

Sachs, Curt. *The Wellsprings of Music.* Ed. by J. Kunst. New York: McGraw-Hill Book Co., 1965.

Schafer, R. Murray. *Composer in the Classroom,* 1965. *Ear Cleaning,* 1967. *The New Soundscape,* 1969. *When Words Sing,* 1970. New York: Associated Music Publishers, Inc.

Soderberg, Janice Rapley. *Development of the Orff-Schulwerk in American Elementary Education.* Master's thesis at San Francisco State College, 1970.

Standifer and Reeder. *Source Book of African and Afro-American Materials for Music Educators.* Contemporary Music Project. Washington, D.C.: Music Educators National Conference, 1972.

Toch, Ernste. *The Shaping Forces in Music.* New York: Criterion Music Corp., 1948.

VII. Drama

Pierni, Creative Dramatics. New York, N.Y.: Herder & Herder, 1971.

Index